PERFECT
ASSESSMENT

for Learning

Claire Gadsby Edited by Jackie Beere

Independent Thinking Press

First published by
Independent Thinking Press
Crown Buildings, Bancyfelin, Carmarthen, Wales, SA33 5ND, UK
www.independentthinkingpress.com

Independent Thinking Press is an imprint of Crown House Publishing Ltd.

British Library Cataloguing-in-Publication Data
A catalogue entry for this book is available
from the British Library.

Print ISBN 978-1-78135-002-7
Mobi ISBN 978-1-78135-027-0
ePub ISBN 978-1-78135-028-7

Printed and bound in the UK by
Gomer Press, Llandysul, Ceredigion

For my beautiful daughter, Poppy Matilda, who gives meaning to everything.

Contents

Acknowledgements iii

Foreword by Jackie Beere v

1. Beware the AfL 'Buffet' 1

2. Sharing Learning Intentions 15

3. Success Criteria: The 'Cinderella' Aspect of AfL 27

4. Engineering Effective Classroom Discussions 35

5. Formative Feedback 49

6. Activating Learners as Resources for Each Other 65

7. Activating Learners as Owners of their Own
   Learning 73

8. Demonstrating Effective AfL Progress to Ofsted and
   Other Stakeholders 83

9. How to Work Effectively with Parents 91

10. Winning Hearts and Minds: How to Successfully Embed
    AfL across the Whole School 97

11. Key Messages: Moving Forward 111

Checklist for Perfect Assessment for Learning *123*

Bibliography *125*

Acknowledgements

Since 2003 I have had the enormous privilege of working as a teaching and learning consultant supporting hundreds of schools. Many of the ideas in this book have been inspired by my work with the committed and talented teachers I have met along the way and who have made me so welcome in their classrooms. I hope this book will be useful to you all. I have tried to give credit where it is due but apologies to anyone who I have failed to acknowledge properly.

Particular thanks are due to the marvellous consultant Janet Evans, Assessment for Learning guru and all-round wonder woman, who has taught me so much about AfL. Also, to my fabulous editor and mentor Jackie Beere who has helped me far more than she should have needed to and who continues to inspire me.

Last, but by no means least, thanks to Kevin, my incredible family and my friends for putting up with me whilst writing this book and for keeping me going in so many ways: I couldn't have done it without you all.

Foreword

Once upon a time there was a land where teachers went into school on a Monday with a couple of bullet points written in their diary with ideas of what they may teach that week. As the week progressed a few annotations may have been added to note what work had been completed and where the learning would go next. The names of children who needed to work a bit harder or could take the lead next lesson may even have been added. Occasionally, an interesting idea about homework tasks may have found its way in. And this, my friends, was my planning diary in 1979.

My results were good and getting better each year I taught. However, I look back in amazement at how random and anecdotal teaching was in those early days. 'Teach one of these texts and let the work grow from there' my Head of Department told me. How different teaching is now – and how much more rigorous is our planning and assessing to ensure our pupils learn effectively. Much of that essential rigour is now delivered through using Assessment for Learning.

If Assessment for Learning is the answer, what is the question?

How can every teacher ensure that every pupil makes progress?

Every child making optimum progress in every classroom in the land is the hope and dream of all those involved in education from Ofsted and the Minister for Education, to the teacher slogging away planning their lessons on a Sunday afternoon. Consequently, teachers ensure that lessons have clear objectives, build in self and peer assessment and include a plenary which measures progress. They also plan their next lesson to ensure progression for all abilities. So what's not to like?

Well, like all prescriptive models of great practice, this can become just a ticklist of ideas to be included in lesson plans. But teachers rarely engage effectively with formative assessment *as* a learning process in the lesson. To really engage with formative assessment you have to be a teacher who has your metaphoric antennae tuned in to what is *really* happening in your classroom. Are those kids *really* engaged with that objective or just writing it down out of habit? Do they actually *know* what progress is in your subject? Or do they just have the customary target sheets stuck in the front of their books with little or no understanding of what they need to do to improve? Do the pupils find that peer assessment really gives them feedback that helps them move on – or does it just give the class know-all an opportunity to remind them how inadequate their handwriting is? Does the plenary really tell the teacher whether every individual child has 'got it'?

Foreword

How can it if the quiet child at the back holds up their whiteboard with the answer on so that the teacher can't properly see it? Is your 'marking' really making a difference to the progress being made over time for every child? Or do they glance briefly at the grade you give them and move on to the next thing?

Just planning to use assessment for learning strategies will not give you an assurance that your lesson is outstanding. You need to really care and get curious about what is happening in your classroom and relentlessly go on a quest to find out – by getting feedback from the pupils and noticing what they are doing. The great strength of this book is that it suggests a huge range of ideas and methods to measure progress and empower pupils to take ownership of their own progress. If you use the myriad of strategies in this book you will grow your instincts about the learning happening inside your classroom. As Claire says, progress happens in their heads – if you can tune in using her techniques you will be helping every child make the most of their ability and using assessment *as* learning.

And that is what I call a happy ending.

Jackie Beere, Tiffield 2012

Chapter 1
Beware the AfL 'Buffet'

Although I am not a gambling woman, I would wager that, if we were to question 100 randomly selected teachers, all of them would at least have heard of Assessment for Learning or AfL. Furthermore, I would bet that the vast majority would be happily using several of the more common AfL strategies such as traffic lighting or peer assessment.

Whilst this is encouraging to those of us passionate about how Assessment for Learning can genuinely transform outcomes for young people, it also alludes to what is one of the great paradoxes: that many well-intentioned teachers are engaging with the letter of AfL rather than the spirit of it. Or, to put it another way, many teachers are grazing at the buffet of AfL without necessarily perceiving how the various morsels come together to form a well-balanced and satisfying educational philosophy.

What is AfL and why does it matter?

Assessment for Learning should not be confused with assessment in its traditional sense; that is, the objective gathering and measuring of progress evidence. Assessment for Learning is much broader and is defined as:

> *... the process of seeking and interpreting evidence for use by learners and their teachers to decide where the learners are in their learning, where they need to go and how best to get there.*[1]

Further exemplification was added in this definition proposed in 2009:

> *Assessment for Learning is part of everyday practice by students, teachers and peers that seeks, reflects upon and responds to information from dialogue, demonstration and observation in ways that enhance ongoing learning.*[2]

Finally, Dylan Wiliam identifies the key elements of AfL as a set of activities which can empower learners to become independent through:

- Sharing learning intentions and success criteria.
- Engineering effective classroom discussions.
- Formative feedback.
- Activating learners as resources for each other.

---

1 Assessment Reform Group, *Assessment for Learning: 10 Principles. Research-Based Principles to Guide Classroom Practice* (Cambridge: University of Cambridge School of Education, 2002).

2 Position Paper on Assessment for Learning, *Paper presented at the Third International Conference on Assessment for Learning*, Dunedin, New Zealand, 2009.

Chapter 1

▓ Activating learners as owners of their own learning.[3]

Assessment for Learning involves asking questions about the quality of learning and being prepared to adapt and enrich the curriculum in response to what we learn. It is important to remember that AfL embodies effective assessment practice which is applicable to all ages, groups and key stages. It has the unique potential not just to measure learning but to promote and further improve learning.

As teachers begin to implement the various practical strategies commonly associated with AfL, such as 'think, pair, share', traffic lighting and peer and self assessment, it is important that they also understand the general principles underpinning AfL. Even busy teachers need to spend time exploring the philosophy behind AfL and constantly ask the question: What does this mean for me and my practice?

AfL is based on constructivism – a view of teaching and learning predicated upon the simple but profound principle that learning is something which can only happen inside the heads of learners. This is why monitoring the 'progress' much sought after by Ofsted can be a challenge – it is often invisible! Also, despite our best efforts as teachers, we cannot make learning happen for our learners – there is a gulf between the teaching and the learning that only the learners

---

3   Leahy, S., Lyon, C., Thompson, M. and Wiliam, D. Classroom assessment: Minute by minute, day by day. *Educational Leadership*. 63(3): 9–24. Available at www.ascd.org/publications/educational-leadership/nov05/vol63/num03/Classroom-Assessment@-Minute-by-Minute,-Day-by-Day.aspx

themselves can bridge in order to develop new skills and knowledge.

Genuine AfL occurs at the point of learning – that moment when a learner engages in personal reflection or interacts with you or another pupil in order to make sense of what is being learned. The most effective AfL practitioners ensure that all of their planning and interactions with learners aim to facilitate exactly this.

In essence, AfL is about empowering pupils to be owners of their own learning. That is to say, learners who can understand where they currently are, what they need to do to improve and exactly how to do this. Clearly, this goes way beyond learners merely knowing their current grade or target or even knowing something about the grade criteria for a particular subject. As Gordon Stobart amongst others observes, real AfL is about learning to learn – a skill for life and not just for examination success.[4]

---

4 G. Stobart, *Testing Times: The Uses and Abuses of Assessment* (Abingdon: Routledge, 2008).

Chapter 1

Is AfL having a 'mid-life crisis'?

Assessment expert Janet Evans recently used the phrase 'mid-life crisis' to describe the current state of AfL.[5] This provocative phrase alludes to the fact that although Assessment for Learning has been around for more than 14 years, and is now supported by a huge wealth of evidence attesting to its positive impact, it is not yet fully or properly embedded in all schools. Reflecting on the table below, why are more schools not yet at the 'enhancing' stage? What are the challenges preventing them from getting there?

---

5   I used the term, 'mid-life crisis' to give a slightly humorous, almost visual, analogy to the idea that AfL had gone through its infancy and reached maturity but had stagnated into a 'comfortable' set of routine, formulaic teacher strategies.

So 'mid-life' was self-explanatory but I wanted 'crisis' to indicate the severity of this implication and the need to take action to change. I invited Gordon Stobart to give a key note there as I'd heard him present at the AAIA [Association for Achievement and Improvement through Assessment] conference (September 2010) using the same phrase of 'a mid-life crisis' so I explained how it had resonated with me. (Janet Evans, AfL and Teaching and Learning Consultant, personal communication, 2012)

Assessment for Learning progression table – where are you?

	Focusing	Developing	
Pupils	All pupils know there are learning objectives. Most know what they have to do, a few have a limited understanding of what they are trying to learn. Some pupils can relate the lesson to recent lessons. Most pupils can work together. Some are confident to contribute to discussions. Some are confident to talk about their work. Most pupils make progress in their learning.	Most pupils are clear about what they are trying to learn. Many are aware of some features of a good learning outcome. Many can, with support, identify some strengths and weaknesses in their work and suggest how to improve it. Many recognise how the learning builds upon earlier learning. In whole-class discussions all pupils listen to others. Many are confident to contribute. In paired or group discussions most pupils contribute and learn from each other. Discussions remain focused. *continues*	

	Establishing	Enhancing
	All pupils have a clear understanding of what they are trying to learn (and value having learning objectives).	All pupils understand what they are trying to learn and confidently discuss this using subject terminology.
	All pupils are clear about the success criteria and can, with support, use these to judge the quality of their own and each other's work and identify how best to improve it.	All pupils routinely determine and use their own success criteria to improve.
	Most pupils can, with support, contribute to determining the success criteria.	Pupils understand how the learning relates to the key concepts and skills they are developing.
	All pupils can relate their learning to past, present and future learning in the subject and most can relate this learning to other subjects.	Pupils value talk for learning and consciously use it to advance their thinking.
	continues	There is a classroom buzz: pupils initiate and lead whole-class discussions; group discussions are self-determined and governed.
		continues

	Focusing	Developing	
Pupils *continued*		Most pupils make progress in relation to the learning objectives.	
Teacher	Lessons are planned to learning objectives and appropriate tasks then identified. The learning objectives and/or learning outcomes are shared, e.g. displayed. *continues*	The lesson is planned to appropriately challenging learning objectives (linked to National Curriculum standards) which focus the teaching. The teacher explains the learning objectives and outcomes and checks pupils' understanding. *continues*	

	Establishing	Enhancing
	In whole-class, group or paired discussions all pupils develop their thinking and learn from each other. Pupils are confident to take risks by sharing partially formed thinking or constructively challenging others. All pupils make good progress, in relation to the learning objectives, with some independence.	Responses are typically extended, demonstrate high-level thinking and support their views. All pupils have an appetite for learning: they independently identify and take their next steps in learning to make good progress.
	The lesson is planned to appropriately challenging learning objectives and intended learning outcomes using success criteria to scaffold learning. *continues*	Planning is informed by an in-depth understanding of standards and progression in key concepts and skills (subject and cross-curricular). The teaching enables each pupil to use AfL to take their learning forward independently. *continues*

	Focusing	Developing	
Teacher *continued*	Opportunities are provided for discussion related to learning (whole class, group or paired). Pupils are encouraged to listen and learn from each other and contribute to discussions. Progress, in relation to the learning objectives, is reviewed with the class, e.g. during the plenary.	The teacher explains what a good learning outcome will 'look like' and this relates to subject standards. The teacher explains the value of what is being learned and how it links to past and future learning (big picture). The teacher relates the tasks to the learning objectives and outcomes throughout the lesson. The teacher regularly assesses learning and provides specific, positive feedback to inform next steps. There are opportunities for structured whole-class and supported group/paired discussion. *continues*	

	Establishing	Enhancing
	Opportunities are provided for pupils to explore the objectives, outcomes and success criteria and sometimes determine the success criteria themselves.	The teacher routinely explores with pupils how they learn most effectively and how this can be applied.
	Exploration of the big picture includes links to other aspects of the subject and to other subjects.	The teacher and pupils develop the lesson together in response to the learning needs.
	Pupils are helped to use success criteria (which focus on fine grades of progression in key concepts and skills) to identify how to take their next steps.	Whole-class and group dialogue is skilfully orchestrated and supported as an integral feature of the lesson to accelerate learning and develop pupils' independence.
	Progress is regularly reviewed with pupils, e.g. prior to the next stage of a task.	Teacher intervention in discussions is minimal but timely and in response to critical learning moments.
	The teaching is flexible and responsive to pupils' learning needs and the progress they are making.	
	continues	

	Focusing	Developing	
Teacher *continued*		The teacher uses specific strategies to improve the quality of dialogue and pupils' confidence.	

So what are the challenges schools currently face surrounding AfL?

1. It may have stagnated as an issue within schools. The fact that AfL has been around for a considerable while means that, in some schools, it is no longer receiving the attention it needs to keep it a 'live' development priority.

2. AfL is not fully understood. It is more than just a selection of exciting classroom strategies. AfL is a philosophy based on the premise of active learning in partnership with learners. Approaches need to be personalised to suit the particular needs of pupils and

	Establishing	Enhancing
	The teacher uses skilful questioning, appropriate resources and engaging activities to focus and sustain whole-class, group and paired dialogue.	
	The teacher explicitly develops pupils' dispositions, skills and confidence to engage in dialogue.	

Source: *The Assessment for Learning Strategy*, 16–17.

this requires an understanding of the wider principles underpinning AfL.

3. AfL is loaded with its own terminology. This can be jargonistic and alienating for some teachers. Although AfL is thought to be understood in almost all English-speaking countries, there is still lots of confusion about exactly what is meant by some of the terminology, leading to confusion within the profession.

4. For AfL to be implemented effectively, teachers need to change their existing practice. This is often difficult as so much of our teaching repertoire is actually subconscious and informed by our own experiences as

learners. Teachers need time and support to make meaning of AfL and this can be difficult in a busy world of competing school priorities and pressures.

These challenges contribute to one of Ofsted's most common findings – that assessment still does not sufficiently inform teaching and learning. Furthermore, Ofsted reports often find that students are unclear about what they are learning and why.

The purpose of this book is to explore these issues in more depth and to offer a range of practical strategies to help schools develop their existing practice and to ensure that assessment really is contributing to learning. The full 'AfL meal' is far more satisfying and effective than random grazing from the buffet. It needs to become so embedded in your classroom that you don't even realise it's what you do every hour, every day and every week to raise achievement.

Chapter 2

Sharing Learning Intentions

If you don't know where you are going, how will you know when you have arrived?

Lewis Carroll

---

8 Schools Project: Key message 1

Fundamental to AfL is that pupils have a clear understanding of what they are trying to learn (learning objectives), how they can recognise achievement (learning outcomes), what 'good' looks like (success criteria) and why they are learning this in the first place (that is, the big picture, sometimes linked to personal curricular targets).[1]

---

1   Department for Education, *Assessment for Learning: 8 Schools Project Report*. Secondary National Strategy for School Improvement (May 2007). Ref: 00067-2007BKT-EN. Available at http://dera.ioe.ac.uk/7600/1/1f1ab286369a7ee 24df53c863a72da97-1.pdf (accessed 1 October 2012), 10.

Sharing learning intentions is all about letting pupils 'in on the game'; in other words, giving them access to the bigger picture. They need to understand not just what is being learned but also to have some sense of why. There is still a lot of confusion around the different terms, especially the difference between 'intentions', 'objectives' and 'outcomes'. Whatever words you use the main message is that your learners understand what learning you hope to achieve together so that they can feel motivated and clear about your high expectations. Key message 1 from the *8 Schools Project Report* is very useful for clarifying the difference for both staff and pupils. This chapter will focus specifically on the crucial role of learning objectives.

An anecdote I often share tells the story of the well-intentioned teacher who, during a departmental meeting held in a classroom, scribbled the following memo on the whiteboard: 'Remember cakes for Jean's birthday on Wednesday'. Imagine her surprise when, the following morning, 32 bright Year 8 pupils copied this verbatim into their exercise books under the heading 'learning objective'. But should she have been so surprised?

Ensure that learners understand and care about the learning objectives

Whilst many teachers claim to feel very comfortable and confident about the fact that they are sharing learning objectives with their pupils, the default model is often pupils simply copying them down. This sort of activity is typically used to 'settle' pupils at the start of lessons and tends to reassure teachers that they have shared the learning objectives. However, as the above anecdote illustrates rather beautifully, such copying actually involves little, if any, engagement with the learning process.

The sharing of learning objectives has, in many cases, become formulaic and Ofsted often report that many pupils do not know enough about what they are learning and cannot articulate exactly what they need to do in order to improve. Many pupils are 'lost in a sea of learning' – surrounded by masses of subject content but unable to navigate their way through it independently.

Another common problem with the sharing of learning intentions is the fact that objectives are often confused with outcomes. Furthermore, objectives can be jargonistic and confuse pupils with too much terminology. Conversely, they can also be diluted beyond recognition by being 'put into pupil speak'. They are often not referred to sufficiently as a planned part of the lesson and all too frequently can become a boring chore rather than a meaningful connection to learning.

At the heart of AfL lies the desire to create genuinely independent learners who can manage their own learning. It invests them with the skills and responsibility they need to make good choices as they negotiate learning challenges. In order to do this, teachers need to make sure that learning objectives are kept 'live' within the lesson by activating them at key moments.

The strategies suggested in this chapter for actively sharing both objectives and success criteria have the added benefit of involving pupils in types of genuinely higher order thinking – such as analysis, classification and evaluation – at points in the lesson which might otherwise have been fairly light in terms of challenge. In other words, they are creating extra challenge for pupils and ensure that there are no lost learning opportunities within the lesson.

This is particularly important in light of the current Ofsted descriptor for outstanding teaching which states, 'When inspectors observe teaching, they observe pupils' learning. Good teaching, which includes high levels of expertise and subject knowledge, with the expectation that pupils will achieve well, enables pupils to acquire knowledge, deepen their understanding, and develop and consolidate skills'.[2] A crucial skill would be to enable learners to reflect on the process of learning as often as possible by developing a 'language' for talking about how they learn. This may include subject terminology or words like reflect, evaluate, compare, contrast, remember, enquire, choose and so on, to ensure they are using a process of metacognition to stand back, think and talk about their learning.

One of the most inspirational head teachers I have met has a school mission statement which reads, quite simply, 'To make learning irresistible'. It is fundamentally important that we deliver lessons which create an emotional hook for our

2 Ofsted, *School inspection handbook*. Ref 120101. Available at http://www.ofsted. gov.uk/resources/school-inspection-handbook-september-2012 (accessed 14 November 2012), 34.

learners. It was Maya Angelou who said, 'People will forget what you said. People will forget what you did. But people will never forget how you make them feel.'[3] For me, an outstanding lesson will always have something which provokes, excites, challenges or moves pupils in some way, and the sharing of learning intentions does not detract from this creative endeavour.

Some teachers, often those from creative or practical subjects, such as drama, art or technology, feel uncomfortable with the idea of revealing the objectives at the start of the lesson in case this spoils the sense of discovery and creativity they are working so hard to create. I am sympathetic to this view and I am not slavish about the need to share them at the very start of every lesson. What is important is that there is *a level of engagement with the learning objective from the outset* of the lesson – even if this is generated in a more indirect way. For instance, a creative approach might be to lead with what I call a 'fascinator' – perhaps an object, an image or a particularly evocative piece of film or music. From this, ask pupils to speculate about what the lesson might be about and, indeed, to see if they can predict what the concealed learning objective is. The 'Rolf Harris' strategy might also be helpful here (see p. 22).

Shirley Clarke helpfully distinguishes between what she calls 'open versus closed' learning objectives, with the difference being that closed objectives tend to lead to fairly limiting

---

3 Quoted in Bob Kelly, *Worth Repeating: More Than 5000 Classic and Contemporary Quotes* (Grand Rapids, MI: Kregel Publications, 2003), 263.

success criteria which can be easily 'ticked off' and don't really allow pupils to demonstrate any great originality or creativity in their work. Open objectives allow for variety of interpretation and give pupils the opportunity to show, and discuss, where they 'did it best'.[4]

Case study

From a teacher using the widely shared WALT (What Am I Learning Today) method.

At first, I have to confess, I didn't really share a WALT or success criteria explicitly with the children. I felt that they would know for themselves what they were learning today simply from the title I wrote on the board and the tasks they were set.

After AfL training I felt I should try some of the ideas that I had learned about, so I would know whether they worked or not and what impact, if any, they might have on the children.

So, for the last few lessons, I explained to the children each time *why* I was showing them the WALT and the success criteria and I asked them for their opinions.

T. Oliver, St. Thomas Boughey High School

---

4   S. Clarke, *Active Learning through Formative Assessment* (London: Hodder Education, 2008).

Long live your objectives!

Please note that the active approaches described in the top tips section below are designed to keep objectives 'live' within the lesson. They rely upon pupils using skills such as prediction, discussion and analysis and are not simply dependent upon learners copying them down at the start of the lesson. You may get your pupils to copy objectives down – at the end of the lesson – but I would urge you to increase the level of challenge by:

- Expecting pupils to recall them from memory (the discussion-based approaches in the top tips below, plus regular reference to the objective within the lesson, should ensure that they are able to do this).

- Expecting learners to add an evaluative comment on their performance alongside the objective (e.g. 'I did this when ...' or 'My best evidence of this is ...').

Top tips for sharing learning objectives with pupils

1. **The pen of power.** Begin by randomly selecting a pupil to come to the front and use the 'pen of power' to highlight key words within the objective and to explain their choices. The important principle here is that it is the learner, rather than the teacher, talking about the objective and annotating it to show their understanding.

I find it is useful to ask learners, 'How would you translate that for a much younger learner?' or 'What are we really trying to do today?' This checks that subject-specific terminology has been fully understood.

2. **The red herring.** Add an extra learning objective and ask pupils at the end of the lesson to identify which one has not been covered and how they know which one was the red herring. The challenge is increased if the objectives are only subtly different, perhaps through changing some of the verbs.

3. **The Rolf Harris.** 'Can you guess what it is yet?' Ask the pupils to suggest what the learning objective could be before revealing it (e.g. it could be completely concealed beneath sugar paper or possibly have just some words visible). Discuss the differences and similarities between pupils' attempts to work it out. Some schools have developed this idea further by hiding the objective behind a pair of stage curtains, either literally or on screen, and finally revealing it with a fanfare and flourish!

4. **Guess who.** Distribute a range of learning objectives to pupils individually and, at the end of the lesson, ask them to work in groups to discuss who thinks they have the correct objective for the lesson in front of them and how they know.

5. **Delete petite.** Discretely delete the objective word by word during the lesson and use these moments as

opportunities to challenge learners to spot which words have disappeared, thus reactivating the objective regularly throughout the session. Challenge pupils to remember the complete objective correctly by the end of the lesson.

6. **Cloze but no cigar.** Present the learning objectives as a cloze activity where pupils are encouraged to fill in the missing words before the completed learning objective is revealed.

7. **Place your bets.** Get pupils to speculate (bid) for verbs that could be used to complete a learning objective (e.g. by using a plenary placemat with key words on it or use Bloom's sentence stems). This method can be used to increase the level of challenge within the lesson as well as engaging the pupils in genuine co-construction of the objective itself.

8. **Mini-plenary.** Incorporate a mini-plenary where pupils are asked to evaluate their progress towards the objectives partway through the lesson.

9. **Translation.** Ask pupils to collaborate to rewrite the learning objectives in a more pupil-friendly style. Next, compare and evaluate the suggestions.

10. **Rank order.** Select two or three learning objectives for the lesson and ask the pupils at the start of the session to vote for the one which they feel is the main class priority.

11. **Nourish deeper learning.** Incorporate one skills-based objective (perhaps a focus on collaborative group work or a personal, learning and thinking skills (PLTS) or social and emotional aspect of learning (SEAL) objective) alongside the subject-based objective. Encourage pupils to think about where else they have used/could use this skill. Indicate if this is going to be the focus for a plenary and, if so, when and how the subject-based objective will be reviewed.

Spot success

Before I showed them a PowerPoint slide with good and bad pieces of work on it (e.g. drawings of some science apparatus). I told them to think quietly to themselves for a moment about what sort of work they felt I would rather see in their books and why. I then explained that looking at the slide was like a game of spot the difference.

All the groups I have shown the slide to (I did the same lesson ten times with different groups) decided that drawing A was the best example and gave good reasons as to why:

'It's neater.'

'They used a ruler.'

'That's scribbled out.'

'The proportions are better'.

I think it had a positive impact. They could see, and were picking out for themselves, the criteria I would be looking for when it came to marking their work. A good follow-up would be to update the examples on the slide with pictures of their own work as soon as possible.

Broken words

I asked my pupils their opinion of how WALTs are displayed around school (before showing them the slide below) and the majority of responses were rather negative:

'The teacher writes it on the board and then leaves it there.'

'We don't really care what it is, we just read it once and that's it.'

'Why do we have one anyway?'

Not overly inspiring feedback! So, with them having expressed their ideas on WALTs, I decided to show them theirs for the lesson:

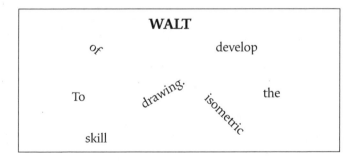

On showing the WALT presented in this manner to the group they virtually all, without prompting, started trying to rearrange the words into a sentence. Some picked up on the clue of the capital letter and the full stop, others just tried to make a sentence by what seemed to be blind trial and error. The pupils all engaged with it more positively rather than simply having the WALT read to them or it just sitting on the board for the entire lesson.

When I asked the groups at the end of the lesson what they had done that lesson and what the WALT was, a few of them remembered it word perfectly so that must indicate on some level that it stayed longer in their memory. Plus, you could argue that it helps to practise the English skills of reading and sentence construction.

The WALT for the lesson was relatively simple (to develop the skill of isometric drawing) so I intend to build on this by maybe giving them either a longer WALT or perhaps two at the same time, which could be easily done if the two sentences were written in different colours. You could write three or even four objectives for the lesson like this.

Chapter 3

Success Criteria: The 'Cinderella' Aspect of AfL

---

8 Schools Project: Key message 2

Pupils' progress is accelerated when they are clear about the success criteria for the intended outcomes and are able to judge the quality of their work and know how to improve it. This requires teachers having a good understanding of progression in the key concepts and skills in their subject.

8 Schools Project: Key message 3

Learning happens in pupils' heads as they assess their level of understanding or quality of their work and recognise how to improve it. This is the essence of AfL.[1]

---

1   Department for Education, *Assesment for Learning: 8 Schools Project Report*, 11.

When we talk about success criteria we are simply describing the detailed breakdown or meaning of the lesson objective. Whilst some sharing of learning intentions is commonplace in many classrooms, it is far less common to see success criteria being used effectively. Does this matter? Actually, it is fundamentally important! As teachers, we know what 'good' work looks like – we carry the mark schemes for most work inside our heads quite instinctively. Indeed, in our marking we tend to use the term 'good' very regularly. But what does this mean?

The mismatch between what teachers mean by 'good' and what pupils understand by the term can be vast. The comments below, taken from a recent work scrutiny, illustrate this perfectly:

Teacher writes (not very helpfully): You must try harder.

Pupil responds: But this is one of my best bits of work because my hand writing is neat, I checked my spellings and I put in the date.

We will explore the implications of this gap between teacher expectation and pupil outcomes more fully in Chapter 5. For now, suffice it to say that you can hear the frustration of both teachers and pupils; a frustration that would have been far less likely to occur had there been a genuine sharing of success criteria within the learning process.

Things would be infinitely easier if all teachers were blessed with telepathic powers and could beam their invisible mark schemes directly into the heads of their learners. Unfortunately, in the absence of this, we need to be much more explicit about our expectations of pupils by the active sharing and, where possible, genuine co-construction of success criteria with them.

In conclusion, the absence of success criteria in many lessons has led me to think of them as the 'Cinderella aspect' of AfL – the neglected relation who has the potential to transform learning into something magical. A few minutes spent really exploring the success criteria with learners could be the key difference in terms of learners making progress.

It is worth remembering that success criteria are most effective when they are staged, which is also a very effective and simple way to support differentiation. Showing learning as a journey with the success criteria for each stage could be helpful (see Jackie Beere's *The Perfect (Ofsted) Lesson* for further suggestions[2]), for example:

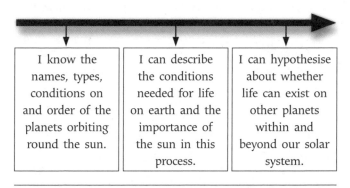

I know the names, types, conditions on and order of the planets orbiting round the sun.	I can describe the conditions needed for life on earth and the importance of the sun in this process.	I can hypothesise about whether life can exist on other planets within and beyond our solar system.

2 J. Beere, *The Perfect (Ofsted) Lesson* (Carmarthen: Independent Thinking Press, 2012).

There is more on this and on how it links to the SOLO model developed by John Biggs and Kevin Collis in Chapter 8.

Try not to impose a ceiling or limit on what pupils can achieve. By leaving a blank box(es) or question mark on the list of success criteria we give pupils the opportunity to add extras and to personalise their learning. It is often more effective to phrase success criteria as 'I am beginning to ...' rather than 'I can ...'

The following strategies may be useful to you in bringing success criteria to life within lessons and many of these can be combined for even greater engagement and interest.

Top tips for bringing success criteria to life

1. **Blankety Blank.** Begin with a blank grid on the board. Invite pupils to suggest what some of the success criteria could be. When, as a class, they have reached agreement about the criteria, each pupil transcribes their own grid which is then referred to regularly throughout the teaching. By giving each criterion a number you can make targeted and formative feedback very manageable (e.g. 'Well done, you have included numbers 1 to 4 very effectively – now see if you can use number 5 in a new paragraph').

2. **Extra, extra ...** Give the pupils a list of possible success criteria plus extras (see 'the red herring' on p. 22). Ask them to suggest which criteria should be deleted and why. This activity involves the higher order skills of

classification and analysis and ensures that pupils are challenged and involved from the outset.

3. **The competition.** Organise learners into groups and challenge them to compile a list of possible success criteria. These can then be critiqued by the class and the 'best' ones selected.

4. **Two for true.** You, or better still a pupil, calls out a selection of possible success criteria. Pupils raise two hands if it is true (a good suggestion) or one hand if it is false (not suitable).

5. **Last man standing**. All pupils begin by standing up. They can only sit down when they have suggested a success criterion. If numbers are an issue, allow the pupils to work in twos or threes. Similarly, if pupils are struggling, allow them a lifeline such as 'pass it to the class' or 'phone a friend'.

6. **In first place.** Give the pupils a range of possible success criteria, either cut up or scattered randomly across a large piece of paper. Ask them to work together to rank order the criteria in order of importance, justifying their decisions.

7. **Building blocks.** For longer term pieces of work, and for younger learners in particular, it can sometimes be useful to build a large-scale display or even a physical model of the success criteria to be displayed prominently in the classroom. You can encourage active engagement

with this in many different ways (e.g. by removing blocks and challenging pupils to remember what was there).

8. **Beat the teacher.** Model the completion of a task (e.g. writing the opening of a creative story, using a material in art or tackling an equation) but with deliberate mistakes. Challenge the pupils to spot where you go 'wrong' and then ask them to correct it. These corrections then become the bones of the success criteria.

9. **Ensure success criteria are displayed prominently throughout the lesson.** These are the key signposts by which pupils can navigate their way towards achievement in each lesson.

10. **Build it up to break it down.** Sometimes it can be advantageous to immerse pupils in the completion of a task without knowing the success criteria for their first attempt. Afterwards, ask them to evaluate the strengths and weaknesses of what they did, thus generating success criteria that can be used to support their second attempt at the task. This might be particularly attractive to teachers of creative and practical subjects who are keen to cultivate originality.

11. **Provide models.** But don't tell the pupils whether you are presenting these as models of good or poor practice. Ask them to analyse and evaluate the models, explaining

their reasons. From this process, pupils can be guided towards generating the success criteria.

12. **Choose your analogy**. Being a terrible cook, I tend to talk to pupils about the 'recipe' for success in my lessons and use cooking related images around my success criteria displays. Other teachers use references to navigation and construction very effectively.

13. **Uplevelling**. Display a weak model and demonstrate how it can be improved. Encourage pupils to make suggestions and incorporate these. If appropriate, pupils themselves can make changes on the board as well as the teacher.

14. **Return to the beginning**. There is extra learning potential to be gained from returning to the success criteria after the work is completed in order to re-evaluate the success criteria (e.g. 'Are we still happy that short sentences always make the best narrative hooks? Explain why').

The most important aspect of sharing learning intentions is to not lose sight of them during the lesson. They need to stay visible and be referred to again and again as part of the session. The success criteria need to be constantly used to measure success during the lesson, in any mini-plenaries and in the final plenary. This diagnostic use should lead to conclusions about 'What do I do next?' and ensures that assessment is genuinely feeding into learning. This is the essence of AfL and is at the heart of the mantra that will help every teacher help every child make progress: 'Know thy impact'.[3]

3   J. Hattie, *Visible Learning: A Synthesis of Over 800 Meta-Analyses Relating to Achievement* (Abingdon: Routledge, 2008), 5.

Chapter 4

Engineering Effective Classroom Discussions

---

8 Schools Project: Key message 4

Classroom dialogue (whole class, group or paired discussion) is at the heart of good AfL as it enables pupils to develop their thinking and to learn from each other. Teachers need to develop pupils' dispositions, skills and confidence to engage in reciprocal talk within a positive climate for learning.[1]

If we are serious in our quest to create genuinely independent learners who are able to interrogate their own learning, identify what they need to learn and support each other, then we need to increase the amount of pupil dialogue in the classroom. There is a well recognised link between talk and the growth of cognitive development. It is through vibrant and structured dialogue that pupils begin to work

---

1 Department for Education, *Assessment for Learning: 8 Schools Project Report*, 11.

collaboratively and enjoy the sense of learning in an active way. Research suggests that dialogue is underdeveloped in many lessons, so AfL simply is not happening – no matter how many strategies the teacher uses.

The latest research suggests that the average lesson is made up of between 70% and 90% teacher input.[2] Whilst we may find this statistic deeply troubling, there are many complex reasons why this figure is so high. Busy teachers talk about the pressure of 'getting through the syllabus' and the fact that 'there is so much to do'. I suspect that, if we are honest, many of us enjoy the traditional teacher role of leading from the front and are at our most comfortable here. For some teachers, classroom discussion can feel threatening as it involves surrendering some of this control. Certainly, dialogic classrooms can feel noisier and more free flowing, but this can be managed by investing time and energy in ensuring that pupils are aware of the protocols and expectations for discussion and group work.

It remains crucially important that we increase the amount of high-level discussion between pupils in schools. Research suggests that 60% of pupils in secondary school never have a conversation with an adult whilst at school. Furthermore, the average length of a pupil response is thought to be five words.[3]

---

2 V. Cook, *Second Language Learning and Language Teaching* (Beijing: Foreign Language Teaching and Research Press, 2000).

3 Professor John West-Burnham and Max Coates *Transforming Education for Every Child: A Practical Handbook* (Network Educational Press Ltd; Spi edition, 2006).

'Literacy includes the key skills of reading, writing and oral communication that enable pupils to access different areas of the curriculum.'[4] The expert panel leading the National Curriculum review has a whole chapter in their 2011 report devoted to its importance, catchily titled 'Oral Language and its Development within the National Curriculum.' The chapter opens by observing that 'There is a compelling body of evidence that highlights a connection between oral development, cognitive development and educational attainment.'[5] We know this, of course, along with the importance of the ability to be able to fluently explain, persuade and argue, but do we know how, or even if, oracy is being taught in our schools? In addition, the report of the expert panel for National Curriculum review recommends that 'the development of oral language should be a particular feature of the new National Curriculum'.[6]

Perhaps, unsurprisingly, research suggests that by the age of just 3 children from less advantaged backgrounds use less than half the number of words spoken by their more advantaged peers.[7] However this 'word poverty' is not only

---

4   Ofsted, *School inspection handbook*. Ref 120101. Available at http://www.ofsted.gov.uk/resources/school-inspection-handbook-september-2012 (accessed 14 November 2012), 12.

5   Department for Education, *The Framework for the National Curriculum: A Report by the Expert Panel for the National Curriculum Review* (December 2011). Ref: DFE-00135-2011. Available at https://www.education.gov.uk/publications/standard/publicationDetail/Page1/DFE-00135-2011 (accessed 1 October 2012), 9.

6   Ibid., 9–10.

7   V. Tuck, Eradicating Word Poverty; Building Word Wealth, *Daily Telegraph* (15 May 2009). Available at http://www.telegraph.co.uk/education/vicky-tuck/5330565/Eradicating-word-poverty-building-word-wealth.html (accessed 1 October 2012).

confined to the less advantaged pupils. It can be best understood with reference to the way that young people today experience the world. We live in a technological age and often interact through technological media. If you watch the typical teenager at leisure, you will probably observe them interacting with smart phones, social networking sites, TV and games consoles – often all at the same time!

That is not to suggest that technology is a bad thing – it can directly enhance learning if used judiciously – but it has radically altered the amount of spoken language used by our learners. It is estimated that in a typical week, a child spends a total of 1,720 minutes watching TV and engaging in meaningful conversation with a parent. Of this, the meaningful conversation with an adult only accounts for 40 minutes or 2.7%.[8]

All of this impacts directly on us as teachers. Robin Alexander identifies five different types of talk:[9]

1. **Rote (teacher-class):** the use of repetition to memorise facts, ideas, etc.

2. **Recitation (teacher-class or teacher-group):** the use of questions to accumulate understanding and knowledge formulated to prompt recollection of previous work, or methodologies.

---

8   S. Kagan and M. Kagan, *Kagan Cooperative Learning*, 2nd edn (San Clemente, CA: Kagan Publishing, 2009).
9   R. Alexander, *Towards Dialogic Teaching: Rethinking Classroom Talk*, 3rd edn (Thirsk: Dialogos, 2006), 30.

3. **Instruction/exposition (teacher-class, teacher-group or teacher-individual):** the delivery of principles, procedures, facts or information to students.

4. **Discussion (teacher-class, teacher-group or pupil-pupil):** the sharing of information and solving problems using the exchange of ideas.

5. **Dialogue (teacher-class, teacher-group, teacher-pupil, or pupil-pupil):** the use of questioning and discussion to develop common understanding in order to develop understanding of concepts and principles, to guide and prompt, reduce choices and minimise risk and error.

His research suggests that discussion and dialogue are seen far less frequently in classrooms. He notes that, 'The issue is not that the first three types of talk are unimportant. Consolidation of work and various routines play a large part in any classroom. What is important is the scarcity, in many classrooms, of dialogue and discussion which, it can be argued, is instrumental in conceptual development and promoting reasoning skills.'[10]

Where classroom discussion does occur, it can be helpful to reflect on what proportion of this is made up of talk about learning and progress as opposed to content. Similarly, we need to ask ourselves what we are doing to create genuine 'basketball' dialogue (team based, with opportunities to dribble – or think – before passing the idea on to someone else who may or may not be the teacher) as opposed to 'ping-

10 Alexander, *Towards Dialogic Teaching*, 30.

pong' dialogue (where ideas are merely batted back and forth between the teacher and one other pupil whilst the rest of the class passively observe).

There is a huge emphasis on questioning in the 2012 Ofsted school inspection handbook:

'Teachers systematically and effectively check pupils' understanding throughout lessons, anticipating where they may need to intervene and doing so with notable impact on the quality of learning.'[11]

Furthermore, inspectors are asked to pay particular attention to the way that teachers respond to pupils' responses. Below are some very effective and challenging questions recently asked of a Year 4 class:

'So, in your opinion, how effective is the author in conveying character so far?'

'Why might that dialogue have been added?'

'Ryan, can you think of a less clichéd word for the lion's noise than roaring?'

Such challenging and targeted questions allowed the teacher to ensure that she was really personalising learning. It is reassuring for busy teachers to remember that effective questions, especially those phrased as plurals (e.g. 'Can you tell

---

11 'Outstanding' descriptor from Ofsted, *School inspection handbook*, 36.

me some of your ideas?') or framed around invitational language (e.g. 'As you will remember ...') are a very quick and easy way to begin to address differentiation in the classroom.

It was John Stuart Mill who argued that we do not learn to read and write, to ride or swim merely by being told how to do it – *we learn by doing it*.[12] Similarly, only by involving children in democratic processes of discussion and decision-making will they ever learn how to practise it.

Case study on the effectiveness of talking chips: Year 8 low ability English lesson

My challenge this year has been to encourage all pupils to take part in the lesson. Many pupils in this group have particularly low self-esteem, thus limiting their oral contributions. At a recent training event Claire mentioned the idea of 'talking chips' – one of Dr Spencer Kagan's cooperative learning structures. Working in groups, each pupil is given two counters, or chips, and can only speak when they have placed their chip in the centre of the table. Pupils should try to link their comments to the one made previously and once the chips are gone, they're gone! Chips can only be redistributed when everyone has used all their chips. It really is amazing how something so simple has transformed my lessons.

---

12 J. S. Mill, *On Liberty* (Harmondsworth: Penguin Classics, 2006 [1859]).

All pupils now contribute to every lesson – but the more I have used this technique, the more extensive their responses have become, which is solely due to an increase in confidence. We've now reached the point where some pupils are using one of their talking chips to challenge (or extend) other's ideas, thus demonstrating excellent listening skills. Pupils themselves have commented that they get greater enjoyment from group work now that certain individuals can't dominate. In terms of the GCSE Speaking and Listening criteria, pupils have to initiate discussion – something the talking chips certainly promote as pupils are desperate to place their chip in the middle of the table before their idea is offered by another group member. Talking chips have transformed my previously reluctant communicators into enthusiastic communicators.

J. Hingley, St. Thomas Boughey High School

Top tips for engineering effective classroom discussions

1. **Group work.** Invest the necessary time to ensure that learners understand how to work effectively in groups. Once you have developed a set of ground rules you can begin to introduce a range of creative group work formats, such as 'jigsaws'. A jigsaw is a grouping strategy in which class members are organised into 'jigsaw' groups. The pupils are then reorganised into 'expert' groups containing one member from each jigsaw

group. The members of the expert group work together to learn the material or solve the problem, then return to their jigsaw groups to share their learning. These approaches help to generate lively discussion.

2. **Push the right buttons.** Ensure that you have an object or topic that pupils will genuinely want to talk about in lessons. Sometimes teachers invest a lot of time and energy setting up discussion tasks which fail to engage the learners. Make use of fascinators, props and so on.

3. **Adequate wait time.** Make sure you build in sufficient wait time before pupils are expected to answer. Opportunities to discuss answers first with a 'talk partner' are vital for extending learning and developing both confidence and interpersonal skills.

4. **Don't jump in!** Practise 'teacher wait time' before responding to pupils. Research shows that many teachers actually answer their own questions or simply rephrase what learners have said. Use a range of non-verbal cues, body language or even symbols or props, rather than words, to encourage pupils to keep talking.

5. **Frameworks**, such as the PMI (Plus, Minus, Interesting) as suggested by Edward De Bono, are useful for extending the range of pupils' thinking and discussion.[13] For example, 'Imagine that all the water in

---

13 See E. De Bono, *Serious Creativity: Using the Power of Lateral Thinking to Create New Ideas* (London: HarperCollins, 1995).

the world is frozen. What would be positive? A minus point? Just interesting? Now put your answers in a table.' The 'interesting' column is especially useful for generating original and divergent thinking.

6. **Use questions which generate emotional connections.** For example, when working with a new class, consider asking them formally about their interests, passions and aspirations and link lesson content and resources to this where possible.

7. **Feedback.** Plan a range of ways of taking feedback. For example, determine the spokesperson at the outset or experiment with giving different groups different tasks so that feedback to the whole class is more purposeful and pupils have a purpose for listening to each other.

8. **Use generic question cue cards.** Try giving cue cards to pupils as they enter the classroom to maximise every child's involvement. They must ask this question of someone (not just the teacher) before the end of the lesson. Questions might include: 'What might someone say who disagreed with that?' or 'Can you back up that idea?'

9. **Randomly select pupils to answer.** Use names on cards or lolly sticks or a computerised random generator. This establishes a 'no hands-up' culture and helps to ensure that all pupils are engaged.

10. **Rank ordering activities.** This is a quick and effective way to get even reticent pupils involved in discussions (e.g. 'Rank these ideas in order of importance').

11. **Introduce 'devil's advocate' or provocative questions.** These give pupils something which elicits a gut reaction or problem to ponder, encouraging deeper thinking and originality.

12. **Questions to generate philosophical thought.** Ian Gilbert's *The Little Book of Thunks*[14] is a brilliant source of questions that are impossible to answer with one word. You might also want to explore Philosophy for Children (P4C) or 'community of enquiry' approaches to generating and exploring 'big' questions.[15]

13. **Questions to explore in depth.** Covering a topic in more detail over a longer time (e.g. the week-long lesson) gives pupils better opportunities to problem-solve and independently apply what they have learned.

14. **Questions to trigger the transference of learning from other subject areas.** For example, 'What can you bring to this from other subjects?' or 'How is this useful in

---

14 I. Gilbert, *The Little Book of Thunks: 260 Questions to Make Your Brain Go Ouch!* (Independent Thinking Series) (Carmarthen: Crown House Publishing, 2007).

15 See www.philosophy4children.co.uk or the Society for the Advancement of Philosophical Enquiry and Reflection in Education (www.sapere.org.uk).

...?' This links to the idea of a competency-based curriculum, PLTS and so on.[16]

15. **Questions which have no single right answer.** For example, 'Did Curley's wife really deserve to die? What evidence is there to support that view?' The teacher may have to model that there is no right answer and demonstrate that we are also learning, alongside the pupils.

16. **Inductive learning activities.** These are particularly effective at promoting independent thought and can be extended using concept-mapping activities. Inductive learning involves presenting pupils with a 'data set' which could be as simple as a series of words or images presented randomly on a page or cut up in an envelope. The task involves pupils organising them into categories which they then name. The important point is that the teacher does not tell the pupils what the categories are. This kind of higher order task involves skills such as classification and analysis and tends to be best tackled in collaboration. Concept mapping, where pupils are invited to move their categories around and to use arrows to explain the relationships between them, serves as a good extension activity.

17. **Questions which allow deeper learning beyond the lesson.** If these are written up in reflective journals, this can be a useful way of encouraging learners to reflect

16 See P. Ginnis, *The Teacher's Toolkit* (Carmarthen: Crown House Publishing, 2001) and Kagan and Kagan, *Kagan Cooperative Learning*.

on their learning journey and also develop extended writing and evaluative skills.

18. **Indirect questions.** This might involve using an image for pupils to investigate, such as a photograph of soldiers in the trenches, and then asking 'What does this tell us?'

19. **Pupil-generated questions.** These can come from pupils using a KWL grid to organise their research, where K stands for 'What do you know already?', W for 'What do you need to find out?' and L for 'What has been learned confidently?' QUADS grids (Questions, Answers, Details and Source) are equally useful.

20. **Questions to close gaps in learning.** One carefully targeted question may allow a pupil to demonstrate progress very quickly whilst developing their vocabulary at the same time. An example of an effective question might be, 'Can you develop your idea a little further using the word *photosynthesis* as well this time?'

21. **Questions as part of a 'conversational classroom'.** Are you happy to be interrupted and questioned by pupils as the lesson unfolds? Do the pupils know this? Do they also know how and when it is appropriate to do this?

■ **Questions which allow answers in any form.** This is another great way of maximising engagement and enjoyment. For example, 'We have been thinking about theories of evolution. Next lesson, can you show me your thoughts? You can use any form including models, pictures and PowerPoint.'

Chapter 5

Formative Feedback

The Ofsted School inpection handbook places great emphasis on the importance of assessment. This is unsurprising given what we know about the power of Assessment for Learning. Particularly interesting is the descriptor for outstanding teaching and learning which reads:

> 'Consistently high quality marking and constructive feedback from teachers ensure that pupils make rapid gains.'[1]

One could argue that this fairly innocuous sentence actually represents a real challenge to teachers. It asks that we regularly engage our learners with assessment in a way that is likely to engage and motivate them, even though they live in the digital age of instant communication which can make so much of our retrospective feedback seem like old news. Can assessment be presented as something exciting and motivat-

---

1 Ofsted, *School inspection handbook*, 36.

ing to pupils? Without doubt it can, but the skill lies in changing the perceptions of both pupils and teachers.

The evidence attesting to the fundamental importance of formative feedback is very clear. John Hattie, whose work draws on a total of approximately 800 meta-analyses, which encompassed 52,637 studies, found that 'the most powerful single moderator that enhances achievement is feedback. The simplest prescription for improving education must be feedback that is "focused, specific and clear".'[2]

Despite all of this evidence, giving good feedback is still problematic. If you perform a Google image search using the words 'marking' and 'feedback', the results you get will look something like the images below. Can you tell which is which?

---

2   J. Hattie and H. Timperley, The Power of Feedback, *Review of Educational Research* 77(1) (2007), 81–112, at 85.

Of course you can! The image of the solitary teacher surrounded by piles of books is reminiscent of the many long hours that I, and most teachers, have spent 'marking'. Far too much teacher time is still swallowed up by marking which, sadly, does nothing to move pupils' learning forward. The reality is that:

- Many pupils do not read the written feedback they are given.
- Teachers tend to write the same comments countless times for the same pupil.
- If feedback is read by the pupil, it is often not understood.
- Even if it is understood, it is seldom acted upon in a meaningful way.

It is an unfortunate fact that many well-intentioned, conscientious teachers are engaged in some marking practices which do very little to help learners make progress. Consider the following example from 6-year-old Jimmy's literacy book:

Well done Jimmy, you can order words in a sentence and can identify initial phonemes.

This comment was probably directed more to Ofsted, the head teacher or even the child's parents rather than Jimmy who, at 6 years old, is unable to read all of the words, let alone understand them. Clearly, these kinds of comments are important markers for us as teachers but perhaps belong in our mark-books – Jimmy needs something else entirely. We need to ask ourselves: Who are we marking for?

The triangle of teacher time

Try to imagine your working time as a triangle and then ask yourself: Where is most of my time spent? The diagram below shows that, for many teachers, marking is a massive devourer of time.

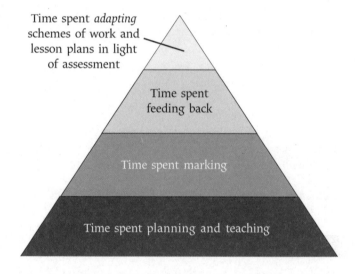

Time spent *adapting* schemes of work and lesson plans in light of assessment

Time spent feeding back

Time spent marking

Time spent planning and teaching

What tends to get far less time and attention is the *active* feedback to learners and the crucial adaptation of planning to ensure that assessment is actively informing teaching and learning. In other words, we are skimping on something vital and we need to redress the balance.

Perhaps we should be marking less often – but much more effectively. We should only give feedback that we know has the power to move learners like Jimmy forward. If you wish to evaluate the efficacy of your current feedback to pupils, it is a good idea to ask them to 'mark your marking'. This simple activity often reveals a profound mismatch between the teacher and the pupil, as illustrated below.

Real teacher comments	How pupils interpreted the comments
You must try harder.	This is one of my best because my hand writing is neat, I checked my spellings and I put in the date.
Develop these ideas further.	How?
Good work – keep it up.	A tick means he probably likes it.
More detail needed here.	What sort of detail?
Use paragraphs.	If I knew how to use paragraphs I would have used them.

However, for all its positives, I would argue that providing effective feedback can be tricky and is something which is not focused on enough in initial teacher training. Indeed, for many busy teachers marking may well be a fairly instinctive process with comments owing much to the kind of feedback that they themselves received as pupils. *Effective feedback is feedback which causes thinking to take place.* The three comments below were taken from a recent work scrutiny. Which of the three remarks strikes you as the most effective in terms of moving learning forward?

> *'Well done. Next time expand your ideas in more detail.'*
>
> *'Very good effort. Have another look at the last paragraph – could you develop your idea further by introducing another quote from the play?'*
>
> *'This is a very interesting story James, but remember to check your spellings!'*

The second comment is much more effective for several reasons. Firstly, it does not use vague phrases such as 'next time' which have little real meaning for pupils and invariably get forgotten. Secondly, this remark provides the pupil with a very specific instruction about how they can immediately act to improve the quality of their work.

Interestingly, the second image, showing 'feedback', represents a very different kind of activity; by its nature it is interactive and collaborative. It implies an active process in which teacher and pupil are both involved in a dialogue, be it written or verbal. One of the best strategies for starting to shift perceptions and practice around formative feedback is to ban the term 'marking'. Instead, place the word 'feedback' at the heart of your work on assessment.

Effective feedback comes in a variety of forms and some of the most effective is verbal feedback given to pupils on a minute-by-minute basis during the lesson. This is what the most effective or agile teachers do: they continuously test the temperature of learning and adapt their teaching accordingly in real time. This is what Ofsted expect:

'Teachers systematically and effectively check pupils' understanding throughout lessons, anticipating where they may need to intervene and doing so with notable impact on the quality of learning.'[3]

Of course, one of the most empowering things for teachers and pupils alike is oral feedback, which intervenes at the point of learning and corrects misconceptions at a stage where pupils can still do something about them. How much more heartening is this than going through a pile of books, each with the same glaring error!

It is important not to let lack of technology become a barrier to providing feedback quickly. Whilst devices such as visualisers (cameras with the ability to connect to virtually any projector, interactive whiteboard, PC monitor or TV screen to

---

3 Ofsted, *School inspection handbook*, 36.

provide a striking visual element to teaching and learning) are fantastic, not all teachers have access to one. Mobile phone cameras can be used just as effectively to capture an image of pupil work which can then be quickly uploaded and explored formatively with, or indeed by, the pupils. Effective feedback is not only crucial because of its massive effect size, but also because it can be very empowering for teachers to know that their time is being well spent.

Language choices are particularly important when it comes to feedback. The word 'but' can be especially damaging to learners' motivation and self-esteem. Instead of 'but' use 'and' to encourage learners to revisit work and to expand their ideas. In the words of Humphrey Walters, 'Getting better never stops'.[4]

Feedback works *both* ways

The most effective feedback is about pupils and teachers working in genuine partnership, and whilst this constructive notion can prove challenging for some teachers, it also represents a real opportunity for teachers to evaluate their current practices and reinvigorate their assessment by working differently. In particular, I am fascinated by John Hattie's observations:

The mistake I was making was seeing feedback as something teachers provided to students – they typically did not, although

---

4   http://www.humphreywalters.com/News/Coca-Cola-ndash-The-Oscas-Daily-Publication.html

they made claims that they did it all the time, and most of the feedback they did provide was social and behavioural. It was only when I discovered that feedback was most powerful when it is from the student to the teacher that I started to understand it better. When teachers seek, or at least are open to, feedback from students as to what students know, what they understand, where they make errors, when they have misconceptions, when they are not engaged – then teaching and learning can be synchronized and powerful. Feedback to teachers helps make learning visible.[5]

It is worth noting that changing the way that you provide feedback to pupils can require careful explanation to parents and other stakeholders (see Chapter 9).

Top tips for making feedback formative

1. **Comment-only marking.** Learners who are given marks as feedback are likely to perceive it as a way to compare themselves with others (ego involvement) whilst those given only comments see it as a way to help them improve (task involvement.) Research indicates that when pupils are given marks alone there is no educational gain at all. Similarly, when pupils are issued with both marks and comments there is no gain. When pupils are provided with comments only there is a 30% gain in terms of pupil achievement.[6]

---

5   Hattie, *Visible Learning*, 173 (my emphasis).
6   R. Butler, Enhancing and Undermining Intrinsic Motivation, *British Journal of Educational Psychology*. 58 (1988) 1-14.

2. **Expect an immediate response to your feedback.**
   Jackie Beere talks about the need for DIRT (Dedicated
   Improvement and Reflection Time) in lessons.[7] Try to
   end your feedback with a specific task for pupils to
   complete or a question for them to answer.

3. **The 'purple pen of progress'.** Make purple the colour
   of progress by providing pupils with purple pens to
   complete their improvements based on your feedback.
   This provides powerful evidence of pupils' ongoing
   progress over time; the more pupil changes and
   additions there are in purple, the more effective you
   know your feedback is.

4. **Make time for feedback.** In the busy world of the
   classroom, staff and pupils are often hurtling from one
   scheme of work to the next with scarcely time to draw
   breath. For feedback to be most effective, it needs to
   have time devoted to it. Try to plan gaps – what I think
   of as 'buffer' or feedback lessons – where quality
   reflection and feedback can take place.

5. **Design a menu of 'feed-forward tasks'.** Pupils should
   complete these in response to your feedback. For
   example:

   ■ Annotate three changes you would have made in
   your work and say why.

   ■ Rewrite a section.

7 Beere, *The Perfect (Ofsted) Lesson*.

■ Look again at success criteria 1 and 6 – now add these to your work.

■ Make six improvements to your vocabulary choices.

■ Annotate your work against the success criteria.

■ Provide another example.

6. **Consider the use of feedback frames.** Try introducing a standard but dynamic format, articulating your expectations of pupils in terms of responding to your feedback. This could take the form of a mnemonic which forms part of your classroom display and expectations:

Read feedback carefully.

Ask if you don't understand what is written down.

Decide which improvement you are going to make first.

Indicate which success criteria you are working on.

Colour of progress is purple – remember your purple pen!

Ask your partner to look at your improvements and to give you honest feedback.

Link your work to the feedback given by your teachers by telling them what you have done and why.

7. **Reverse horseshoe forum.** Give status to feedback sessions. For instance, try to create a different mood and feel to the lesson by changing the layout of the room. I like to use what I call the 'reverse horseshoe

forum' in these lessons. In this model, the pupils sit on the inside of a horseshoe arrangement facing away from each other and the teacher and engaging in independent work. The role of the teacher is to move around the outside of the horseshoe providing one-to-one oral feedback and guidance to pupils. Clearly, some pupils will need more of your time than others and it may take a little practice to ensure that independent work and pupil behaviour allow you to work effectively in this way. Do not feel constrained by the room layout (you may find your own method) or assume that you need to use this approach all the time. The important thing is to ensure that pupils sometimes get to explore their work with you face to face. As one pupil said to me recently, 'I want to talk about my work with the teacher, and not the other way round.' This approach provides just such an opportunity.

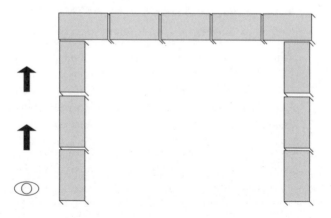

8. **Use guided work.** This is an ideal model for working closely with targeted pupils to help them improve their work in response to your feedback.

9. **Oral-only feedback.** John Hattie's research acknowledges the large effect size of working one to one with learners. This is a very labour intensive and costly way of teaching. However, by linking it to a short feedback conversation (perhaps as part of a horseshoe forum lesson) you can yoke two of the most effective pedagogies together at the same time. Time and again, I come back to research which suggests that 60% of pupils never have a proper conversation with an adult whilst at secondary school and it is rare to find a pupil who is willing to admit the fact that they are struggling to understand what their teacher has written on their work. This approach makes it more likely that learners will understand individualised feedback from their teacher or seek clarification.

Oral feedback can be based on notes that you have made whilst reading and reflecting on pupils' work, but sharing it orally makes it much more immediate and effective. Teachers who recently trialled this approach then asked pupils to make their own notes based on what had been discussed. These comments were then dated and verified by the teacher. Feedback from the students involved indicated strongly that they thought this was an effective way of receiving feedback and, interestingly, they felt that they took more notice of the formative comments when they wrote them down themselves.

10. **4x4 feedback.** This is a pedagogy for bringing feedback into teaching itself. The title refers to the four activities of: *exploring* an anonymous/exemplar response, *guessing* the feedback/mark that would go with it (based on the success criteria), *modelling* how to improve it and, finally, *inviting* learners to do the same with their own work.

11. **Delayed gratification.** Young people live in a digital world of instant communication. Sometimes it can be advantageous to defer their expectations around feedback. You might mark work in the usual way but, rather than writing comments on the work itself, write them on a separate piece of paper, preferably placed in a sealed envelope. Give back the work and explain that the pupils will get their personalised feedback at the end of the lesson. During the lesson itself, engage pupils in feedback activities such as 4x4 feedback before 'revealing' your feedback to them at the end of the session. Engagement and understanding of the feedback is optimised because of the way learners have engaged with the process during the lesson.

12. **Feedback margins.** This is a designated place on the right hand side of the page where you can genuinely begin to create a two-way dialogue with pupils in which you can hear and respond to their feedback to you.

13. **'Two stars and a wish' and 'Even better if ...'** These make very useful frames for feedback but overuse can lead to them becoming formulaic. Invite pupils to help you design new, class-specific models that they will be even more likely to engage with.

14. **Link classroom display to feedback.** For example, against your large-scale display of success criteria, get pupils to generate a quick 'progress bite' or implementation task, perhaps on a sticky note, which they place next to the criterion they think they have evidenced. (See Chapter 8 for more on progress bites and demonstrating pupil progress.) This makes assessment literate pupils an everyday reality in your classroom, demonstrates progress over time and keeps the learning 'live' for pupils between lessons.

15. **Beware the phrase 'next time' when marking.** This has very little meaning for learners unless we are going to apply specific dates and times. Far better to allow immediate opportunities for pupils to respond to feedback whilst it is still in their minds.

16. **Make marking imperative.** For example, 'Change three adjectives to improve the impact of your work.'

17. **Sticky notes.** These are a fantastic way to provide instant formative feedback to students without interrupting them (e.g. 'Great Gemma, now use another quote from the play to develop your idea further' or

'Well done on checking the success criteria – have another look at number 4').

18. **Insist that pupils respond to your feedback**. You can encourage this by structuring marking in the following way:

 What Went Well (WWW) – Positive aspects of the work.

 Even Better If (EBI) – Action needed to improve.

 My Response Is (MRI) – Pupil writes a response to the feedback or just signs up to above action.

Chapter 6

Activating Learners as Resources for Each Other

What the child can do in collaboration today, he can do alone tomorrow.

Lev Vygotsky

Dylan Wiliam's five elements of AfL are at the heart of effective teaching and learning. However, whilst almost all teachers agree that these features are fundamentally important, they sometimes struggle to pinpoint what they might look like in practice. Furthermore, they struggle the most when it comes to the final two:

- Activating pupils as resources for each other.
- Activating learners as resources for themselves.

As challenging as they may be, these two principles are fundamentally important to effective AfL. The old adage states that 'classrooms are where pupils go to watch teachers working hard' and there remains more than an element of truth to this. As discussed in Chapter 3, the average lesson is made up of between 70% and 90% teacher input which is clearly not conducive to developing pupils as active participants in their own learning. This chapter will address the first of these points and the next chapter will deal with the second.

The best lesson I have ever observed took place in a school with an opening minds/ learning-to-learn ethos where pupils were explicitly taught how to be active learners. The Year 7 science lesson in question not only had maximum pupil engagement and participation, it also had minimal teacher input from one very relaxed teacher whose role was to act as a genuine 'guide on the side' as pupils navigated themselves through the lesson.

It is important to bear in mind that, in a fiercely competitive employment market, EQ (emotional intelligence) and inter-personal skills are now often thought to rank more highly than traditional IQ. Creating the right kind of classroom culture can allow these skills to be cultivated. However, as far back as 1998, Black and Wiliam noted that 'It requires hard and sustained work to overcome this pattern of passive reception.'[1] This, unfortunately, remains true – but it can be overcome.

---

1   P. Black and D. Wiliam, *Inside the Black Box: Raising Standards through Classroom Assessment* (London, GL Assessment, 1988), 10.

Chapter 6

Peer assessment

'Consistently high quality marking and constructive feedback from teachers ensure that pupils make rapid gains.'[2]

Peer assessment is advocated very strongly in the latest
Ofsted inspection handbook and many schools are familiar
with the principles and advantages of peer and self assessment. Where one encounters teachers who are reluctant to
engage in peer assessment this is often due to a fear that
pupils might not be accurate enough in their judgements or
be unnecessarily generous or harsh. Evidence suggests that
this is not the case and that pupils are perfectly capable of
providing high quality formative feedback to each other when
they have access to success criteria and feedback models/
frames.

At its best, peer assessment allows pupils' work to become a
subject of genuine discussion between themselves:

*Engaging in peer and self assessment is much more than just
checking for errors or weaknesses; it involves making explicit what
is normally implicit, and thus requires pupils to be active in their
learning.*[3]

---

2 'Outstanding' descriptor from Ofsted, *School inspection handbook*, 36.
3 P. Black, C. Harrison, C. Lee, B. Marshall and D. Wiliam, *Working Inside the
   Black Box: Assessment for Learning in the Classroom* (London: NFER Nelson, 2002),
   15.

Black et al. go on to claim that, 'Peer and self assessment makes unique contributions to the development of pupils' learning. They secure aims that cannot be achieved in any other way.'[4] Exploring exactly what those aims may be can provide a very productive discussion for both staff and pupils alike. One proven benefit is that pupils are much more likely to seek clarification from and, indeed, challenge each other than they would the teacher.

However, peer-to-peer feedback can be very tokenistic and, at its worst, is merely pupils politely complimenting each other using generic phrases such as 'Well done'. The skill of effective feedback needs to be explicitly and consistently modelled and taught by teachers across the curriculum.

Of course, activating learners as resources for each other encompasses more than just peer assessment. It is about a classroom culture of collaborative learning where the teacher is happy to share responsibilities and roles with the pupils and where discussion and group work are prevalent.

It is worth noting that although learners are often organised into groups within classrooms, research indicates that within these groups learners' interactions are frequently ineffective.[5] Indeed, there is a big difference between working *in* groups and working effectively *as* groups. Learners need to be taught the conventions and expectations of effective group work

---

4 Ibid., 15.
5 M. Galton and J. Williamson, *Group-Work in the Primary School* (London: Routledge, 1992).

before they can act most effectively as resources for each other.

Top tips for activating learners as resources for each other

1. **Talk partners** are crucially important and should be randomly generated and rotated after no more than one week for maximum impact.

2. **Spotlighting** is a particularly powerful way of evaluating the collaborative work happening in the classroom.[6] When pupils are engaged in group work, periodically ask them to pause, signal that it is 'spotlighting time' and then ask one group to resume its work while a metaphorical spotlight is shone on them. The role of the rest of the class is to observe and be prepared to offer formative feedback as required.

3. **Day-to-day classroom routines** can be used to develop pupils' interpersonal skills and general ability to support one another without needing to ask the teacher. Think about introducing classroom roles which are rotated (e.g. a door monitor to meet and greet, a book monitor or a designated pupil to scribe on the board for the teacher). These small changes have a cumulative effect and help to establish a culture where pupils begin to look to each other as well as the teacher for guidance.

---

6 See the Royal Shakespeare Company, *The RSC Shakespeare Toolkit for Teachers* (London: Methuen Drama, 2010).

4. **Use a random name generator** to determine which learners are going to provide feedback or talk about their own work. You can download software onto your computer or just use a jar full of name labels.

5. **Cooperative learning (Kagan structures).**[7] Embrace pedagogies which are specifically designed to promote the development of pupils' interpersonal skills. Approaches like the cooperative learning structures advocated by Dr Spencer Kagan provide an opportunity to develop subject-specific learning, interpersonal skills and emotional intelligence at the same time using one activity. What one could describe as a 'buy one, get one free' pedagogy!

6. **Take over the teaching.** Introduce the expectation that, once a pupil has successfully completed their work, they make themselves available to help others in the group. This is particularly effective in practical subjects where 'pupil helpers' circulate the room offering support. Be careful to ensure that pupils understand that their role is to coach others – not to complete the work for them.

7. **The spectacles of feedback.** To really signal the importance of peer assessment, and the expectation that pupils should be assuming a different role, I encourage pupils to make their own 'feedback glasses'. Using the 3D cardboard glasses issued by cinemas as a template, I invite pupils to make and customise their own pair.

---

7   See Kagan and Kagan, *Kagan Cooperative Learning*.

Putting these on prior to assessing either their own or their partner's work really focuses attention and improves the engagement of younger pupils.

8. **Film stars.** Experiment with filming learning as it unfolds in the classroom. This footage provides brilliant opportunities for pupils to see how best to evaluate each other's work and can be used to show the difference before and after feedback has been given. Photographs can be used in much the same way.

9. **Put the words into their mouths.** Work with your pupils to design a bank of effective feedback comments available for them to use. These could be laminated and placed in pots in the centre of tables.

10. **Group-generated questions.** Ask pupils to work in groups to write down five questions and, following whole-class discussion, identify the best two from each group. This generates 10 or 12 good questions which can be explored possibly as homework.

11. **Anonymous models.** Use examples of work from anonymous pupils and ask their peers to suggest possible ways of improving the work and how they would meet the learning outcomes.

12. **Question time.** Ask pupils to work together to write their own questions and in addition to provide answers to each other's questions.

13. **Make sure peer assessment mirrors the best practice modelled by teachers.** For example, peer assessment should be followed by an immediate opportunity/ expectation that pupils do the feed forward/improvement task.

14. **Don't confine pupils to just written peer assessment.** Make full use of oral feedback but perhaps capture comments on thought-bubble shaped stickers for future use/reference.

Chapter 7

Activating Learners as Owners of their Own Learning

'Teaching promotes pupils' high levels of resilience, confidence and independence when they tackle challenging activities.'[1]

The need to create independent learners has never been greater. The current Ofsted school inspection handbook is peppered with references to pupil independence – and with good reason. Research from as early as 1992 suggested that the world in which our young people were going to grow up was even then changing four times faster than the average school.[2] Furthermore, we are preparing our young people for life in what is currently a difficult financial climate globally

---

1 'Outstanding' descriptor from Ofsted, *School inspection handbook*, 36.
2 Research by Dr William Daggett cited in G. Dryden and J. Vos, *The Learning Revolution: To Change the Way the World Learns* (Visions of Education) (Stafford: Network Educational Press, 2001).

and a fiercely competitive job market nationally and interna-
tionally.

Young people need to be able to operate successfully in an
increasingly globalised world. Psychologist Herbert Gerjuoy
of the Human Resources Research Organization phrases it
simply: 'The new education must teach the individual how to
classify and reclassify information, how to evaluate its verac-
ity, how to change categories when necessary, how to move
from the concrete to the abstract and back, how to look at
problems from a new direction – how to teach himself.
Tomorrow's illiterate will not be the man who can't read; he
will be the man who has not learned how to learn.'[3]

As teachers, parents and educationalists we have a moral
imperative to help our young people to develop the crucial
skills of independence, flexibility, responsiveness and, above
all, resilience. To be a successful 21st century learner, pupils
need to have these skills nurtured from the early years of
education in order for them to be fully embedded by school
leaving age. Assessment for Learning has a huge contribution
to make.

Constructivism is a view of teaching and learning based on
the simple but crucial premise that learning is something
which can only happen in the heads of learners themselves.
We cannot, despite our best efforts, simply transplant content
and skills into the heads of our pupils.

---

3   Cited in A. Toffler, *Future Shock*, (London: Pan Books, 1973), 271.

A widely circulated cartoon by Bud Blake shows a young boy declaring of his dog, "I taught Stripe how to whistle". A sceptical friend notes, "But I don't hear him whistling". The boy retorts, "I said I taught him to whistle, I didn't say he'd learned it".

Instead, our energies are best directed at ways of supporting our pupils in learning *how* to learn. Teachers, as well as learners, need to see *learning as part of the curriculum*. Without the right school and classroom ethos, which recognises the importance of thinking and learning skills, many of our AfL endeavours are destined to fail.

When the going gets tough, the tough get going ...

Carol Dweck's seminal research on mindsets reminds us of the need to cultivate learners with a growth, or mastery, mindset.[4] In other words, cultivating learners who value learning and are both resilient and determined when they encounter challenge or failure. This resilience comes from the fact that learners with a growth mindset believe that effort leads to success and that they have the capacity to improve. Learners with a growth mindset are able to gather themselves when faced with difficulties and talk themselves through tricky situations – a crucial skill for learning and for life.

---

4   C. Dweck, *Mindset: The New Psychology of Success* (New York: Ballantine Books, 2007).

Hence, teachers who are effective at assessing where pupils are in their learning, and who are able to articulate these levels of attainment followed by 'next steps' advice on improvement, will engage pupils in their learning in a positive way and increase their self-motivation to learn and achieve.

This approach produces particularly impressive learning gains when working with less able pupils as it reduces their anxiety of failure and, instead, creates an environment where everyone is able to move to the next stage in their learning. For more able pupils, this strategy encourages further learning as it does not put a ceiling on achievement, as a grade does, and instead signposts for learners their next learning goals. It also teaches that 'there is no failure, only feedback'.

Another adage reminds us that 'failure is a great teacher'; it is fundamentally important that pupils learn through active participation and 'doing'. The recent Functional Skills initiative[5] suggested a model of learning which showed learners moving smoothly between the building phase of learning (usually teacher led) to the applying stage (practical application) before progressing to the stage where skills are securely mastered.

However, experience suggests that, for most learners, the transitions from one stage to another are far from smooth.

---

5 Functional Skills are qualifications in English, maths and ICT that have been available in England since 2010. They are designed to help learners build the practical skills necessary to get the most out of work, education and everyday life.

Indeed, learning can often look more like a journey across the famous red balls from the television show *Total Wipeout*, fraught with challenges and frequent falls!

In addition to the growth mindset characteristics described by Dweck, pupils need access to high quality learning objectives and success criteria in the short term, and meaningful targets in the mid to long term, in order to be able to clearly see where they are on their own learning journey. It is also clear that classroom routines and structures have a key role to play in fostering pupils' independence. Classrooms with significant levels of independent learning, contrary to many teachers' expectations, tend to be much more structured. They have clear procedures for everything and pupils understand how to operate.

In addition, it is worth giving careful consideration to *how* information is conveyed to pupils. Try to make sure that success criteria or classroom expectations are always generated in partnership with the pupils and communicated in language which is as accessible as possible.

Case study: PE

It was excellent to see a group of pupils – who had previously been quite difficult to motivate in theory lessons – remain on task and enthusiastic throughout. They loved the starter activity of Kagan's 'Jot Thoughts' where they had to work together as a team but independently of the teacher. The challenge was to remember and record as many things as they could from the previous lesson. They thrived on the competitive nature of the challenges set and when 'the spies' were sent out from each group they became very protective of their knowledge and appreciative of the knowledge of those around them.

It was effectively such a simple starter activity, yet it set the tone for the entire lesson, encouraging an atmosphere of challenge and independence which ultimately led to excellent progress and an 'outstanding' observation.

H. Goodwin, St. Thomas Boughey High School

Top tips for activating learners as owners of their own learning

1. **Pause points.** Younger learners do not instinctively reflect on and edit their work during the process. Often their main focus is task completion. Without disturbing their creative flow and absorption in the task, try to create 'pause points' for pupils to reflect on their work in progress. You could experiment with a subtle sound signal, a countdown or a flashing visual prompt, which invites them to pause and carry out a reflection task at a suitable moment.

2. **Reflection tasks.** These can be laminated and displayed around the classroom, placed in pots on tables or stuck into books. Like feedback tasks they may be more memorable if presented as mnemonics such as:

   Cream of the crop?

   Come to a stop.

   Read what you have produced so far.

   Evaluate your work against the success criteria.

   Ask yourself: 'Is this my best effort?'

   Make one small change before carrying on.

3. **Lesson domestics.** These can be used to actively encourage independence. Try experimenting with book monitors, a choice of materials or tasks for pupils to choose from, pupil-generated displays or pupil-led plenaries.

4. **Pick up where we left off.** Ensure that pupils can catch up easily if they have missed a lesson. For example, take a screen shot of the key learning each lesson, print off copies and display prominently in the classroom. Encourage pupils to take a copy and discuss with a friend or the teacher.

5. **The guide on the side.** The teacher acts as a facilitator and pupils are expected to talk more than they are. The teacher is in yes/no answer mode and, during independent work, they will only provide yes/no answers or say 'pass to the class' so that difficult questions are directed to the class.

6. **Tap into the talent in the room.** Instead of the teacher providing input in the early stages, begin by drawing out what pupils already know by getting them to seek out information from each other. Challenge pupils to talk to six different class members in order to find out six pieces of knowledge or ideas about a particular topic. This works especially well at the start of a new topic or as a revision activity.

7. **Pupil annotation of their own work.** 'I did this because ...' This is a very powerful way of gaining an insight into the deeper learning of particular pupils. This kind of annotation is most effective when it relates directly to success criteria and provides teachers with a sense of exactly what the pupil was thinking during the process of completing their work.

8. **Regularly and routinely involve pupils in actual lesson delivery.** This can be done by choosing pupils at random to present their homework or revision to the rest of the class who, in turn, provide feedback based on the success criteria.

9. **Teach from the back.** Simply changing your position within the classroom dramatically alters the dynamics of the lesson as the pupils are not automatically looking for input from the teacher at the front of the room but are using independent learning strategies. Interestingly, it also physically repositions the teacher into more of a facilitator role.

10. **Devil's advocate or provocative statements.** Giving pupils something which elicits a gut reaction or asking them to ponder a problem encourages deeper thinking and originality.

11. **Getting unstuck – the 'B strategy'.** Instead of stepping in and providing the pupils with the answers to difficult questions, model ways for them to get themselves 'unstuck'. For example: check your **B**ook, **B**oard, **B**rain and **B**uddy before you ask the '**B**oss'!

12. **Talk timer for teachers.** Most teachers are used to setting time-managed tasks for pupils. Try setting the timer and stating explicitly: 'I will introduce the topic for the next 10 minutes only, and then it's over to you to apply what you have learned.'

13. **The week-long lesson.** This could mean studying a topic in more detail to allow pupils to problem-solve and independently apply what they have learned.

14. **Pupils taking responsibility for designing their own learning.** Ask students: 'If this is our objective, what suggestions do you have for how we might learn it?'

15. **Question cue cards.** These are generic questions that are issued to pupils at the start of the lesson. It is the responsibility of the learners to ask the questions of each other during the session, thus reducing the amount of teacher talk.

16. **Creating a culture of 'no single right answer'.** Try setting lessons as problem-solving exercises (e.g. 'Was Henry VIII a good king?'). The role of the teacher is to

model that there is no right answer and that we are learning alongside our pupils.

17. **Reflective journals.** These can be a useful way of encouraging learners to reflect on their learning journey plus they also develop extended writing and evaluative skills.

18. **Inductive learning activities.** These are particularly effective at promoting independent thought. Inductive learning involves a data set (which could be as simple as a selection of words and/or symbols presented in a random order) which pupils must sort into sub-categories. The crucial thing is that the teacher should not specify how many categories there are or what they should be called.

19. **The silent lesson.** This creates both intrigue and real concentration. Display a problem, question or 'fascinator' (see Chapter 3) on the board and then invite the pupils to respond – but don't use any words! This takes practice; focus on an engaging stimulus, mime and passing on the pen to pupils to take over.

20. **Plenaries and self-assessment.** These are ideal places to promote further independence. Begin by asking learners to tell you what they have learned, rather than us as teachers telling them what *we think* they have learned.

Chapter 8

Demonstrating Effective AFL Progress to Ofsted and Other Stakeholders

'Much of the teaching in all key stages and most subjects is outstanding and never less than consistently good. As a result, almost all pupils currently on roll in the school, including disabled pupils, those who have special educational needs and those for whom the pupil premium provides support, are making rapid and sustained progress.'[1]

Progress has become a particularly prevalent term in education in recent years – and necessarily so. Effective teaching and learning must surely result in pupils making progress. And some pupils – those 'gap' pupils who show up in blue on your data – need to make exceptional progress. Progress and assessment are always likely to be key features of an

---

1 'Outstanding' descriptor from Ofsted, *School inspection handbook*, 36.

inspection handbook and are certainly at the heart of the 2012 version with its emphasis on 'rapid and sustained' pupil progress. In a real sense, the current Ofsted inspection hand-book is Janus-faced – looking both backwards and forwards to understand and evaluate pupils' learning journeys. Inspectors are particularly interested in pupils' books as evidence of progress, so all that has been taught and learned previously is also being inspected.

It is very common to encounter teachers who are anxious about pupil progress and, specifically, how to evidence this. Progress can be tricky to substantiate because you can't demonstrate progress if none is taking place, not all progress is adequate progress and it can be hard to recognise, define and communicate to others.

However, there is good news. Effective embedded assessment for learning can give teachers the confidence to regularly 'check the temperature of learning' and then adapt the learning to suit individuals and pupil groups more accurately. This may manifest itself in annotated lesson plans showing the changes that teachers are making, based on the knowledge they have gained from assessment of their pupils. During inspections, formative assessment of progress will be obvious in the quality of classroom dialogue and, particularly, in the way that teachers respond to pupils' responses. Furthermore, a sense of progress will be palpable when pupils are able to articulate their understanding of the learning they are involved in and point to success criteria and formative feedback that is helping them to move forward. In other words,

Chapter 8

outstanding lessons are those in which pupils are fully assessment literate, to use John Hattie's phrase.[2]

A key finding of the 8 Schools Project was the fact that, although progress during individual lessons resulted from a complex set of factors, evidence suggested that it was most significant when:

▨ Objectives were limited in number and focused.

▨ The success criteria for the intended outcome(s) were shared and understood by all pupils towards the beginning of the lesson.

▨ There was high quality whole class interactive teaching involving effective teacher questioning and quality dialogue.

▨ Pupils were given opportunities to improve their work either against success criteria or in response to feedback (teacher and/or peer).

▨ Underpinning the above factors, teachers had a clear understanding of progression.[3]

In *The Perfect (Ofsted) Lesson*, Jackie Beere uses a continuum as a tool to help teachers and pupils recognise learning as a journey and that they need to move forward to make progress[4] (see also Chapter 3). This has been used successfully with some teachers as a way of differentiating and

2 Hattie, *Visible Learning*.
3 Department for Education, *Assessment for Learning: 8 Schools Project Report*, 30.
4 Beere, *The Perfect (Ofsted) Lesson*, 19–20.

demonstrating the cognitive development required for deep learning.

A popular way of supporting deep learning is the SOLO taxonomy which many teachers are using to show pupils how to strengthen their understanding and apply learning to new contexts, as in the figure below.

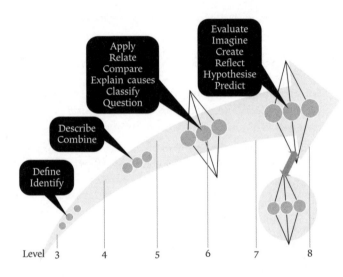

Based on J. B. Biggs and K. F. Collis, *Evaluating the Quality of Learning: The SOLO Taxonomy* (New York: Academic Press, 1982).

Learning can start at any point on the arrow and move up and down. For example, you need to define and identify the planets before you can create a really effective hypothesis about UFOs, or you can start with the hypothesis and then unpick the facts and figures that may give you evidence to prove your case.

In conclusion, as professionals teachers know when their pupils are making progress and can draw on assessment evidence and mark-books to illustrate this over time. However, it can be rather more problematic to demonstrate that pupils are making progress *within* an individual lesson. The following strategies may be useful.

Top tips for demonstrating pupil progress

1. **Set appropriate learning objectives.** Check that these are skills-based and sufficiently challenging and engaging. Try to explore them in an interactive way with pupils (perhaps by using 'the pen of power' annotation). Ensure that they are returned to throughout the lesson thus keeping them 'live' for learners. Pupils will then have a reference point for thinking or talking about their progress at any given moment to a visitor.

2. **A recipe for success.** Check that pupils have access to success criteria within each lesson. These function as a recipe or map showing pupils precisely *how* to progress in their learning.

3. **Portable plenaries.** These can be dropped into a lesson at any point to allow you to gauge pupil progress. Interactive strategies such as 'last man standing' and 'two for true' are particularly effective. 'Last man

standing' involves all pupils standing up before being invited to sit down when they have contributed something to the discussion of what has been learned. Oral rehearsal with a partner first plus a 'phone a friend' lifeline ensure that this is not damaging to pupils' self-esteem and confidence. 'Two for true' involves you, or better still a pupil, reading out a statement about the learning. The pupils raise either two hands for true or one for false. This kinaesthetic activity is very engaging and provides you with a very quick but accurate picture of pupil understanding.

4. **Targeted questioning.** This has a key role to play – the random generation of pupil names to answer questions helps to ensure that all learners are fully engaged.

5. **Progress points in classrooms.** These can be very helpful in signposting pupil progress by making it very visible to all. Strategies such as KWL (what do we **K**now, **W**hat do we need to find out, what has been **L**earned confidently), QUADS (**Q**uestions, **A**nswers, **D**etails, **S**ource) grids, 'graffiti walls' and 'post-it/park-it walls' can also be used interactively in the lesson itself.

6. **Progress bites.** In other words, quick implementation/ application tasks to demonstrate that pupils have grasped the main learning point. This could be a timed paragraph, equation or question which, again, can be dropped into a lesson at any point and would serve to provide a portable plenary.

7. **The killer question.** Make a point of asking pupils: 'What do you know/can you do that you didn't/couldn't do an hour/week/month ago?' Then ask them to respond to this in a variety of ways – verbal, written, diagrammatic or physical.

8. **Explain it to a 5 year old.** Asking pupils to simplify and synthesise their learning in order to explain it to a much younger pupil really exposes any gaps in their learning.

9. **Fill in the gaps.** Try presenting pupils with an overview of the lesson/unit in the form of a cloze activity. This could take the form of individual pupil versions or a giant display which pupils independently fill in when they are confident that they know the answers.

10. **Transposition or transformation of learning.** By asking pupils to present their learning in a new way we can begin to see shades of understanding. For example, ask pupils for a metaphor (e.g. If this topic/idea was an object it would be a ... because ...). Pupils can also represent their learning in the form of models, movement and so on which can be easily captured in photographs.

11. **Podcasts or sound bites.** Catch them being clever and keep this evidence safe using a Dictaphone or mobile phone (e.g. 'Who would like to have a go at summing up what we have learned so far in one sentence that we can record?'). This sort of classroom culture actively

encourages pupils to develop their vocabulary and speaking skills.

12. **The power of peer and self assessment.** This is well documented. Pupils' own responses to their work can be supported by grids containing success criteria which they can link to their own work. Crucially, this allows them to talk in specific detail about their targets rather than superficial comments such as 'I need to get to level 5'.

13. **Ask a big question.** This would be an *overarching question*, maybe straddling several lessons, which could be displayed in the classroom. At any point you could ask pupils: 'What do you feel that we know now that would help us to answer this question?'

Chapter 9

How to Work Effectively with Parents

The vast majority of parents care deeply about how their child performs at school. However, even more important to the average parent is the question of how their child feels about school. Are they happy? Do they feel safe? Do they feel cared for by their teachers? The great thing about effective AfL is its potential to address these concerns. Not only is AfL proven to have a profound impact on pupils' learning, it also, by its nature, develops interpersonal and communication skills as well as resilience. The personalised support offered to pupils via formative feedback also celebrates the child as an individual. All of this is good news but the challenge remains: How can we convey this most effectively to parents?

Schools have changed dramatically since many of us were pupils. What we now know to be best practice in terms of assessment is likely to be very different from what most parents experienced when they were at school. Often, on a subconscious level, the average parent is probably expecting to see their child's exercise book covered in red pen with plenty of ticks and a liberal sprinkling of ubiquitous comments such as 'Well done!' and 'Check your spellings'. The biggest potential problem is that parents also want to see grades and marks and this is at odds with best AfL practice.

As discussed previously, the holy grail in AfL terms is the pupil who:

- Understands their own learning journey.
- Pinpoints what it is they have done successfully and what they still need to improve.
- Articulates this knowledge when asked by parents or other interested parties.

Schools that, with the best of intentions, attempt to embed AfL practices without clearly explaining to parents how and why are likely to encounter real resistance from parents who perhaps feel that marking is not being done in the 'proper' way or often enough.

In order to avoid this try using the feedback approaches detailed below. In my experience of working with many schools, the vast majority of parents are very supportive of AfL – but only after these kinds of changes are explained carefully to them first.

Top tips for working most effectively with parents

1. **A PR offensive.** Research suggests that a significant percentage of parents find schools intimidating due to

their own experiences as pupils. Try offering interactive and fun workshops which demonstrate that learning, and assessment, has altered dramatically since they themselves were pupils – and for the better! Ensure that parents experience a range of learning activities alongside their children so they can see for themselves the power of AfL.

2. **A Trojan mouse.** We all know that it can be particularly difficult to engage certain parents and these are often the ones we most want to reach. If you cannot entice parents to take part in the kind of sessions described above, try a more stealthy approach by dropping AfL type strategies and messages into the more well-attended events such as sports day and annual concerts.

3. **A radical rewrite.** Have an honest look at your existing policies around assessment and then rewrite them in a shorter, illustrated and straightforward way, avoiding jargon and acronyms, and share them with parents.

4. **Manage expectations.** In pupils' books and planners include a short and explicit statement of what parents can expect in terms of assessment, and stick to this.

5. **Make research resonate for parents too.** In this statement include a short overview of what the overwhelming weight of research tells us about the efficacy of formative feedback. John Hattie's work on effect sizes might be useful here.

6. **Consistency of practice.** Ensure that staff in all subject areas follow the same policies and procedures in terms of marking and feedback to avoid confusion on the part of parents.

7. **Use success criteria effectively within lessons.** Then make sure that pupils have copies of these in their books, making it easy for parents to see exactly what their child has been learning and how and why feedback is being attributed.

8. **Design a feedback key.** This helps consistency and should outline the range of different types of feedback and how often they might be used. For example:

   OF = Oral Feedback given

   PA = Peer Assessed

   SA = Self Assessed

   TA = Teacher Assessed

   TAA = Teaching Assistant Assessed

   GF = Group Feedback given

   PTF = Pupil Transcribed Feedback (teacher feedback which has been transcribed by the pupil)

9. **Be upfront.** Research shows that parental involvement in children's education from an early age has a significant effect on educational achievement, and continues to do so into adolescence and adulthood.[1] Tell this to parents – it is a powerful incentive for them to get more involved.

---

1   The Impact of Parental Involvement on Children's Education, 2008. Ref DCSF – 00924-2008BKT-EN.

10. **The right tools for the job.** Inform parents about their unique potential to develop their child's learning but be crystal clear about exactly how they can do this. Provide the questions you would like them to ask their children, such as 'What do you need to do to improve in subject X?' or 'Do you have success criteria you can show me?'" Most powerfully, get parents to ask their children to 'show me where you did it best'. Try to encourage a regular engagement with parents in the assessment process, perhaps by identifying a feedback margin/ section of the pupil planner or exercise book where parents are invited to provide comments and/or questions related to the work. Tell them it is OK to write their own comments and questions in pupils' books.

11. **Develop assessment literate parents.** Post copies of mark schemes, success criteria and annotated model answers online so that you create assessment literate parents as well as pupils.

12. **Parent assessment.** Encourage not only self and peer assessment but parent assessment as well. Experiment by providing parents with a list of effective feedback comments in the same way that you might for pupils (see Chapter 6) and encourage them to make use of these when working with their children.

13. **Use the 'purple pen of progress'.** (See Chapter 5.) This provides powerful visual evidence that feedback from pupils, teachers and parents is actually contributing to pupils' progress.

14. **Make it personal.** The best way to get parents involved is to extend a personal invitation. General letters or flyers home tend not to be overly successful – try to create ways to communicate with parents one to one.

15. **V is for visibility.** Try to ensure that you are communicating your ethos and expectations around assessment using the fabric of the school. For example, make sure that displays around the building, and especially in the foyer, celebrate work in progress as well as finished pieces, and that they feature AfL strategies and success criteria.

16. **Drip feed.** Continuously reiterate the importance of AfL using all the means at your disposal. Pepper your leaflets, newsletters and other publications with key quotes about AfL research and the power of effective feedback and parental involvement. Similarly, capture photos or film footage of pupils engaged in peer assessment and use these to enhance your website/ learning platform.

17. **Pupils' annotation of own work.** This provides even the most sceptical of parents with powerful evidence that assessment for learning really does empower their children to take control of their own learning and to make progress.

18. **Parent View.** Once they are all onside, encourage them to say how brilliant your school is on Ofsted's Parent View.

Chapter 10

Winning Hearts and Minds: How to Successfully Embed AfL across the Whole School

There is no doubt that teaching is hard work. There is a relentless drive for raising standards in education and an ongoing expectation that all schools should be engaged in continual school improvement activities. This places a huge burden on schools and, particularly, senior managers who must decide with which initiatives and agendas to engage. It is not uncommon to hear teachers talk about 'initiative overload' and to encounter cynicism about new ideas. Interestingly, ideas that teachers haven't generated for themselves are often what they perceive as overload. Busy teachers need to know what's in this for them and their pupils.

It is important to remind ourselves that AfL is not all new. Effective AfL practice has always been part and parcel of good teaching and learning, and indeed, many teachers will have been using some AfL strategies successfully even before the term Assessment for Learning was first coined. Perhaps some of the resistance from teachers stems, in part, from all the jargon and acronyms prevalent in education. In light of all of the massive educational initiatives over the last decade, including the National Strategies, there is a danger that AfL has been overlooked or dismissed as just another such prescriptive acronym or passing trend. We need to remind ourselves that Assessment for Learning is about one core thing: developing independent and resilient learners who are in charge of their progress.

As we know, schools are complex and ever-shifting landscapes where staff (and priorities) change over time. What I call the 'C Cluster' is helpful for remembering that any successful whole-school development work is dependent upon senior leaders having a real awareness of:

- Change management
- Cultures
- Collaboration
- Classrooms

Successfully developing Assessment for Learning involves change and, like any other change, this will need careful handling. Asking teachers to alter their practice involves asking them to step outside of their comfort zones. Historically, teaching has been a private endeavour with individual teachers labouring in their individual classrooms, whereas Assessment for Learning calls for an open and flexible approach to the process of learning that becomes a partnership with pupils.

The most successful schools tend to have a culture of collaborative working, often with teaching and learning communities (TLCs) at their heart. Leahy and Wiliam recommend that teaching and learning communities should consist of eight to ten classroom teachers in the same school who have committed themselves to embedding formative assessment techniques in their teaching.[1] They also suggest that teachers need to engage with colleagues in a TLC for at least two years in order to change habits and see improvements in pupils' learning.

In essence, the principles of experiential and collaborative learning that we want for our pupils needs to be replicated by the staff. The latest research from the Centre for the Use of Research and Evidence in Education certainly shows that one of the most powerful types of continuous professional development (CPD) is staff learning from and with other teaching colleagues.[2]

In a very real sense, what pupils need, teachers need. When we ask teachers to describe the best professional development they have ever had, it is interesting to note that many will struggle to remember a single CPD experience clearly. Interestingly, if you ask those same teachers to recall a

---

1   S. Leahy and D. Wiliam, *Embedding Formative Assessment. Professional Development Pack 2 for Schools: Teacher Learning Communities in Action* (London: Specialist Schools and Academies Trust/Schools Network, 2010) [CD-ROM].

2   Centre for the Use of Research and Evidence in Education, *Mentoring and Coaching CPD Capacity Building Project: National Framework for Mentoring and Coaching* [n.d.]. Available at http://www.curee-paccts.com/files/publication/1219313968/mentoring_and_coaching_national_framework.pdf (accessed 1 October 2012).

particularly memorable lesson from their own time at school, they will probably do so accurately. The learning experiences which stay with us for life tend to be those that were unique, unexpected or emotional or those which challenged our world view in some way. We need to think about creating CPD opportunities with more of these components.

Schools with various achievement-raising projects and live action research projects which interrogate their practice, tend to cultivate a professional dialogue where continuous school improvement is inevitable. However, it may be the case that the individuals who champion initiatives such as AfL are working in relative isolation and can easily get worn down – hence the need for TLCs.

Whilst classrooms have been shown to have three times more direct impact on pupil outcomes than anything which happens at school level,[3] the challenge of moving on classroom practice remains. Perhaps one of the reasons is the fact that teachers are busy people often working in a highly pressurised environment and cannot be expected to embrace new ideas and practices merely on recommendation. In the words of Black and Wiliam:

> *Teachers will not take up attractive sounding ideas, albeit based on extensive research, if these are presented as general principles which leave entirely to them the task of translating them into everyday practice ... What they need is a variety of living examples*

---

3   B.P.M. Creemers, *The Effective Classroom*. (London: Cassell, 1994).

of implementation ... and to see concrete examples of what doing better means in practice.[4]

In conclusion, initiatives often fail in schools due to the fact that insufficient time and energy is devoted to them. Thus hearts and minds are not won over sufficiently to change the habits and beliefs of the teachers. For AfL this is due, in part, to a range of factors including:

- A lack of understanding about AfL and belief in its impact.
- A lack of sharing and networking of effective practice within and across subjects.
- Competition with other priorities.
- Contradictory policy and practice within the school leading to a lack of consistency.
- A lack of focused, coordinated and supported CPD.

Often, the most promising starts fizzle out because other priorities or everyday workload divert attention. The key point to remember is that, unlike some other fashionable initiatives that come and go on a frequent basis, Assessment for Learning has proven to be an investment worth making, as you will have seen in earlier chapters.

The 8 Schools Project, which looked in detail at exactly how schools had successfully embedded AfL, made the following recommendations about effective whole school development

---

4   Black and Wiliam, *Inside the Black Box*, 15–16.

work. (Key messages 1 to 4 relate directly to classroom practice and are discussed elsewhere in this book.)

Key message 5

Effective whole school change must be informed by a thorough and on-going analysis of the overarching learning needs of the pupils. This is about diagnosing common obstacles to learning in lessons and teachers working collaboratively within and across departments to address these. Pupils' learning needs change over time as schools help their pupils develop as learners.

Key message 6

To establish AfL whole school both 'top down' and 'bottom up' change processes must prevail as they fulfil different purposes. 'Top down' approaches can convey a clear message about expectations and focus for improvement but this alone does not win the 'hearts and minds' of all teachers or build internal capacity.

Key message 7

AfL practice is most successfully developed where teachers work collaboratively within and across departments, share their practice and learn from what they and their peers do well. Change is most effective when there is a sustained professional dialogue between teaching staff and between staff and their pupils. In planning change, consideration needs to be given to establishing mechanisms for encouraging and facilitating this dialogue.

Key message 8

Senior and middle leaders need to maintain an unrelenting focus on, and support for, the intended change. This includes addressing the issue of competing priorities and the contradictory practices which may stem from these.

Key message 9

A secure and shared understanding of what effective AfL practice 'looks like' is essential for teachers to be able to reflect and develop their practice and for leaders to be able to help them do this. Isolated pockets of good practice can be developed by individual teachers but, for AfL to have significant impact, development needs to be whole school. Everyone, especially senior and middle leaders, must continue to develop a more insightful understanding of AfL.

Key message 10

Senior and middle leaders need to reflect critically on their ways of working; they should flex and change through learning from others to take intelligent informed risks. Effective leaders are able to both continue to refine and sharpen their current approaches to whole school change and introduce new ones where things are not working.

Key message 11

The whole school development of any pedagogical approaches, and associated teaching strategies, requires systematic and systemic monitoring and evaluation of the impact of this on:

- The quality of teaching and learning;
- Standards;
- The leadership and management of change.

Key message 12

Monitoring and evaluation needs to be a distributed process involving all teachers and subject teams. It should be enquiry-based and inform continuing professional development (CPD) (e.g. ongoing action research in lessons and coaching). CPD is a journey not a series of isolated events.

Key message 13

Pupils can provide rich and penetrating evidence and
insight into what works well in lessons and what doesn't.
Engaging pupils in school self evaluation also helps them
develop as reflective learners and practitioners in much
the same way as it does teachers.[5]

Fundamentally, the biggest challenge is how to move from
the 'inspiration' stage (often associated with a dynamic
INSET session or launch) to the genuine 'implementation'
stage where good practice in Assessment for Learning is fully
embedded across the whole staff.

The following tips may be useful to you as you review how
to embed Assessment for Learning in your school.

Top tips for winning hearts and minds

1. **Make it personal.** Try to establish an emotional
   connection between staff and the notion of AfL. A
   useful activity may be to invite teachers to choose an
   image or metaphor which sums up what outstanding
   teaching and learning means to them. Opportunities to
   really talk about our own educational philosophies are
   very rare but are crucially important to a profession
   which is subject to so many external influences and

---

5 Department of Education, *Assessment for Learning: 8 Schools Project Report*, 13–14.

expectations. From this discussion, next ask staff to think about the components which would make up their ideal classroom and feed in AfL principles as part of this discussion.

An image that represents learning as a process of constant amending, refining, nurturing, perfecting and selecting would work well for AfL.

2. **Go back to the basics.** To begin with, ensure that all staff are aware of the bigger picture about what Assessment for Learning is and why it is so important. (The research evidence cited in this book will help you to do this.)

3. **Know where to start.** AfL has been around for more than 14 years so it is likely that most schools will have made a start on engaging with it and pockets of good practice will probably exist. It is important to assess your staff and find out where they are in relation to AfL. The AfL progression tables (see pages 6–13) may be useful in establishing where you currently are.

4. **An audit by any other name.** Think of a *creative* way to ascertain teachers' knowledge of, and commitment to, AfL. You could try asking staff to self-categorise by aligning themselves with a statement they most identify with.

5. **Incidental CPD.** Maintain a momentum and buzz around AfL by placing what I call 'tantalisers' in the

vicinity of teachers. These could include snippets of key research with key words missing displayed in the staffroom or visually striking teaching props (e.g. the brightly coloured and eye-catching timers manufactured by Ballotini) dotted around to remind staff about the prevalence of teacher talk in classrooms.

6. **Differentiate.** Staff will need to be re-engaged with AfL in different ways. Consider targeted sessions and offers (e.g. top-up workshops for some staff and classroom-based coaching for others). Where possible, try to include an element of choice by saying, for example, 'Over the course of the year, everyone will be invited to take part in three AfL CPD opportunities, one compulsory and two of your choice from this selection.'

7. **Problem-solving.** Invite staff to share a perennial 'problem' with assessment that makes their life difficult (e.g. pupils not reading feedback) and experiment with solutions for a short period of time.

8. **Make it very visible.** Perhaps introduce a staff learning wall where staff are encouraged to post ideas and strategies they have used. (It can be helpful to incentivise this – perhaps by issuing a raffle ticket for each contribution with a prize draw every Friday.)

9. **Own it.** Of course, AfL will look and feel very different from school to school. By generating an attractive and eye-catching 'product', such as a placemat or poster, which collates real examples and photographs of AfL

work undertaken in your school, you are effectively customising it for your context. This kind of central reference document is especially powerful when it contains both staff and pupil evaluations and is very useful for ensuring that any new staff members are fully conversant with the school's expectations around assessment.

10. **A radical rewrite of your assessment policy.** Look at what latent assumptions are lurking in your current and possibly outdated version. Challenge these, then rewrite it so it is shorter, more purposeful and links to success criteria. Put this in every classroom or teacher planner.

11. **Keep AfL at the centre of your day-to-day business.** Make AfL the first standing item on the agenda for any meeting and perhaps encourage departments to introduce 'ten minute Tuesdays' (a ten minute slot where they informally share their ideas and reflections on what they have trialled recently in classrooms).

12. **Tell me a story.** Provide time and space for staff to 'tell the story' of their classroom-based work. According to Mark Friedman, telling stories is one of the oldest ways of making sense of the world and converting our own experiences into useful lessons. It allows each person to express their unique perspective on a situation.[6]

---

6   M. Friedman, *Trying Hard is Not Good Enough* (Oxford: Trafford Publishing, 2005).

13. **Continue to invest time and resources in high-quality CPD.** But give careful thought to the design of INSET sessions: 'INSET needs to provide new experiences, support the anxieties which accompany not just the threat but the genuine difficulties of change and give people time to reflect, work things out and think things through.'[7] The most common complaint from teachers following INSET sessions is lack of time for follow-up and implementation.

14. **Collaboration.** Wherever possible, actively support staff to work together to trial new approaches in the classroom. The 'Lesson Study' model[8] where staff work closely in pairs to design strategies, deliver them and observe each other, is particularly effective. It involves looking closely at the specific impact of certain strategies on the learning of three pupils who are identified in advance. The fact that the observing teacher is clearly focused on the three pupils makes the observation far less threatening and personal.

15. **Involve all major stakeholders in the process.** Pupils will become powerful advocates for AfL once they recognise the difference it makes to their own learning.

---

7   B. R. Joyce and B. Showers, *Student Achievement through Staff Development* (White Plains, NY: Longman, 1995), 13; quoted in A. Harris, *School Improvement: What's In It for Schools?* (London: Routledge-Falmer, 2002), 100.

8   Department for Children, Schools and Families, *Improving Subject Pedagogy through Lesson Study: Handbook for Leading Teachers in Mathematics and English* (October 2009). Ref: 00937-2009BKT-EN. Available at https://www.education. gov.uk/publications/eOrderingDownload/Improving%20subject%20 pedagogy%20through%20Lesson%20Study.pdf (accessed 1 October 2012).

Formally notifying parents about important changes to marking and assessment will pay dividends in the long run, as best practice AfL may look and feel different to what many parents may expect based on their own education. (See Chapter 9 for more on how to work most effectively with parents.)

16. **Incorporate AfL into performance management.** Make it a key priority for everyone, every year, until it is embedded. Use coaching to help those who are not moving forward with it and, if necessary, use sanctions such as capability procedures or withholding movement up the pay spine.

17. **Use lesson observations or drop-ins to embed AfL.** Prior to these ask teachers, 'Which aspects of AfL would you like me to look for specifically in your lesson?'

18. **Let AfL lead your marking policy.** Ensure that progress over time is evident in pupils' books, that they respond to written feedback and that there is a consistent language children use about their learning.

Chapter 11

Key Messages: Moving Forward

Tell me and I'll forget,
Show me and I may remember,
Involve me and I'll understand.

Chinese proverb

Chapter 1 – Beware the AfL buffet

Assessment for Learning is now well into its second decade and the vast majority of teachers probably know something about it and may even be using some of the strategies most commonly associated with AfL, such as traffic lighting or peer assessment. However, AfL is much more than just a set of appealing classroom strategies and is, in fact, an educational philosophy based upon the idea of active learners constructing meaning for themselves.

In a recent article in the *Times Educational Supplement*, Dylan Wiliam expressed disappointment at the fact AfL had not progressed as far as it might have.[1] Wiliam attributes this in part to the actual title 'Assessment for Learning' which perhaps does not make clear enough that it is really all about *learning*. Perhaps the name AfL has led to an over-emphasis on the 'Assessment' in terms of measuring and checking, and not enough focus on the crucial phrases *'for* Learning'. Indeed, one of Ofsted's most common findings is that assessment does not sufficiently inform teaching and learning.

The time is right to revisit and revitalise AfL. Busy teachers need to be reacquainted with all of the powerful components of AfL rather than just nibbling at the edges of some of the more appealing strategies.

Moving forward ... Use the AfL progression tables on page 6 to take an honest look at how embedded AfL is in your own practice or your school.

Chapter 2 – Sharing learning intentions

A common Ofsted finding is that many pupils are often unclear about what they are learning and why. For effective learning to take place, learners must understand not just *what* they are learning but *why*. They need the big picture. Whilst many teachers are familiar with the idea of sharing learning objectives with the pupils, the default model is often

---

1 See W. Stewart, Think You've Implemented Assessment for Learning?, *TES Magazine* (13 July 2012). Available at http://www.tes.co.uk/article.aspx?storycode=6261847 (accessed 1 October 2012).

to copy these from the board or to frame them in a very formulaic way.

Moving forward ... The active sharing of lesson objectives – and success criteria – adds a further element of challenge and engagement. Ensure that in any lesson the objective is *actively* explored and discussed with learners and is then kept 'live' within the lesson. (See page 22 for 'The Rolf Harris' and other practical suggestions.)

Chapter 3 – Success criteria: the 'Cinderella' aspect of AfL

Success criteria are the lesson objectives broken down into manageable steps. These serve as an effective 'recipe' for learners to use within their learning and help to ensure that both teachers and learners have the same understanding of what is expected as an outcome. Not only is this empowering for learners, it also means that teachers are less likely to get unpleasant surprises when work is handed in and learners haven't succeeded in the way they had hoped.

Moving forward ... Success criteria should be clear and easily understood. Learners should also be involved in generating these and should be able to see them displayed within the lesson. (Try 'Extra, extra!' or one of the other practical strategies on page 30.)

Chapter 4 – Engineering effective classroom discussions

Teacher input is thought to account for between 70% and 90% of the average lesson. Clearly, if learners are to be active participants in, and co-constructors of, their learning they need to be able to talk! It is through discussion and dialogue that learners can make the necessary connections in their learning and begin to internalise and shape their knowledge.

If we are serious in our quest to create genuinely independent learners who are able to interrogate their own learning, identify what they need to learn and support each other, then we need to increase the amount of pupil dialogue in the classroom. It is through vibrant and structured dialogue that pupils begin to work collaboratively and to sense and enjoy the learning in an active way. Research suggests that dialogue is undeveloped in many lessons so AfL simply is not happening – no matter how many strategies the teacher uses.

Moving forward ... Make pupil dialogue a key development point for INSET. Monitor pupil dialogue in lesson observations and share strategies that work.

Chapter 5 – Formative feedback

John Hattie extensively reviewed a total of about 800 meta-analyses, which encompassed 52,637 studies, and concluded that effective feedback is *the* most powerful tool for moving learners forward. Opportunities to provide effective feedback exist throughout the course of each and every lesson. The use of targeted questions and mini-plenaries allow teachers to ascertain what has been learned and to adapt the lesson in response.

Written feedback is labour intensive for teachers and evidence suggests that pupils often fail to engage with it in the way that we would hope. In some cases this could be due to a lack of interest on the part of pupils; after all, once a piece of work is completed it can feel pointless and frustrating to return to it. Alternatively, learners may struggle to understand what has been written or what is expected of them. Teachers need to ensure that feedback always 'feeds forward'. In other words, ensure that feedback is specific and positive but also indicates precisely what needs to be done in order to improve.

There is an overwhelming body of evidence attesting to the fact that comment-only marking is the most effective and that grading does not work. A shift in practice is required which may be difficult for some staff, pupils and parents to understand. The rationale for moving to this will need to be explained.

Moving forward ... Ensure that for every piece of written feedback given to learners, teachers expect a response from pupils – and make time for this to happen within the lesson. The 'purple pen of progress' is an easy and effective mechanism for getting learners to engage with feedback and make real improvements to their work immediately. (See page 58 for this and other practical ways to make feedback more effective.)

Chapter 6 – Activating learners as resources for each other

At the centre of the AfL classroom is the learner rather than the teacher. As educators we have a moral imperative to equip our learners to be successful in the world beyond the school gates. Success in this real world environment is dependent upon interpersonal skills such as effective communication, team work and emotional intelligence. All of these crucial skills can be developed and honed in the day-to-day classroom environment. Peer assessment has an obvious and sizeable contribution to make, but can be developed further.

Moving forward ... Train your teachers in the skills of peer coaching so that they can teach the learners how to coach each other (see *The Perfect Teacher Coach*[2]). In addition, 'spotlighting' is a fantastic and fast way of encouraging learners to act as critical friends for each other. (See page 69 for this and other practical ways to activate learners as resources for each other.)

---

2   T. Broughton and J. Beere, *The PerfectTeacher Coach* (Carmarthen, Crown House Publishing, 2013).

Chapter 7 – Activating learners as owners of their own learning

AfL is based on constructivism, a view of teaching and learning centred on the simple but crucial premise that learning is something which can only happen in the heads of learners themselves. We cannot, despite our best efforts, put the learning into place for our students. Instead we need to create learning environments with autonomous, self-motivated learning at their heart.

The more we can support learners to master the actual skills of learning, the more they will be able to manage it for themselves. In effect, we need to teach learners *how* to learn most effectively and to value learning itself as part of the curriculum. The following all have a key contribution to make:

▒ Effective classroom routines

▒ Pedagogies

▒ Limiting the amount of teacher talk

Moving forward … Use the 'B strategy' (see page 81) consistently across the curriculum to encourage resilience amongst your learners and to teach them effective ways of getting 'unstuck' when learning becomes difficult.

Chapter 8 – Demonstrating effective AfL progress to Ofsted and other stakeholders

Progress is a complex commodity. The 2012 Ofsted 'outstanding' descriptor for teaching calls for 'almost all pupils' to be 'making rapid and sustained progress'.

Pupils are most likely to make progress when:

- They understand what progress means within individual lessons and can navigate this for themselves using lesson objectives and success criteria.
- They feel consulted and they are able to influence and shape their own learning.
- They are fully engaged in the lesson and use a language for learning.
- The lesson has motivational content and activities as well as sufficient challenge.
- They have ample opportunities to engage in dialogue and collaborative work.
- They have access to high quality feedback and opportunities to make improvements to their work.

Teachers are professionals; they know when their pupils are making progress and can draw on assessment evidence and mark-books to illustrate this over time. However, it can be rather more problematic to demonstrate that pupils are making progress within an individual lesson or to showcase pupil progress most effectively.

Moving forward ... Consider the use of motivational 'progress bites' (see page 88) to enable pupils to demonstrate their learning and progress in the short term rather than just at the end of lessons/unit tasks.

Chapter 9 – How to work effectively with parents

Education in general, and assessment in particular, has changed considerably since most parents were pupils themselves. Many parents will still expect to see marks and grades but implementing AfL involves comment-only marking. Work will be necessary to ensure that parents understand not just what has changed in marking but *why* it has. Parents' attitudes about learning and assessment have a direct impact upon the views of their children and so it is worth investing time to make sure they are fully informed. A feedback key is a powerful way of communicating to parents the rich variety of feedback their children will experience as part of AfL.

Just as Hattie argues for the need to have 'assessment literate pupils', we also need to ensure that we have 'assessment literate parents' who are conversant with the relationship between success criteria, formative feedback and feed-forward tasks, as well as the importance of resilience and motivation on the part of the learner. This is fundamentally important as parents are uniquely placed to help their children learn if given the tools and opportunities to do so.

Moving forward ... Help parents to help their children learn more effectively. (See 'the right tools for the job' and other practical strategies on page 95.) Run regular workshops for parents to show them how to support their children's learning. Publish a handbook for all parents to be distributed for each key stage.

Chapter 10 – Winning hearts and minds: how to successfully embed AfL across the whole school

Successfully embedding AfL across a whole school is dependent upon effective change management and the acknowledgement that each teacher has their own unique set of values and beliefs about education. Busy staff need support and encouragement to try out new approaches in their classrooms and cannot be expected to embrace novel ideas merely on somebody else's recommendation.

As a school, focus on embedding one aspect of AfL at a time. There is a lot of terminology associated with AfL and it is not uncommon to encounter confusion around terms such as *objectives* versus *intentions*. Use less terminology but ensure that staff have a genuine and shared understanding of any terms that are introduced.

Too many initiatives wither and die in schools due to lack of sustained attention and commitment. It is estimated that any whole-school initiative takes approximately five years to become fully embedded: quick wins simply don't exist if we want real change. Teaching and learning communities which meet regularly have been found to be one of the most effective ways of embedding AfL across a whole school.

Moving forward with AfL is an ideal opportunity to revamp how continuing professional development and training looks and feels in your school. Link AfL initiatives to the new teacher standards and to performance management strategies; formative assessment is clearly identified as central to improving teaching and learning.

Moving forward ... Experiment with new ways of refreshing AfL in your own school, perhaps using 'incidental CPD' or one of the other practical strategies on page 106.

In conclusion

Assessment for Learning has a massive potential to improve outcomes for learners. When teachers use minute-by-minute and day-by-day assessment to adapt their teaching more precisely to learners' needs, achievement and engagement are maximised. To embed this requires more than just the introduction of a few new teaching strategies. In the words of Christine Harrison, 'assessment disappears into teaching and learning when it is done well'.[3]

---

3 C. Harrison, keynote address at the Optimus Assessment for Learning conference, June 2012, London.

Checklist for Perfect
Assessment for Learning

AfL progression tables on page 6 are used to look at how embedded AfL is in your own practice or your school. ✓

The lesson objective will be actively explored and discussed with learners. ✓

Success criteria are clear and easily understood. ✓

The whole class will be involved in lesson observations and strategies that work will be shared. ✓

Written feedback is given to the learners and time allowed for feedback with the teacher. ✓

You will acquire the skills of peer coaching and you teach the learners how to coach each other. ✓

The 'B strategy' is used consistently across the curriculum to encourage resilience amongst your learners and to teach them effective ways of getting 'unstuck' when learning becomes difficult. ✓

Motivational 'progress bites' will be used to enable
pupils to demonstrate their learning and progress in
the short term rather than just at the end of lessons/
unit tasks. ✓

Parents are assisted in helping their children learn
more effectively. ✓

New ways of refreshing AfL in your own school are
continually investigated. ✓

Bibliography

Alexander, R. (2006). *Towards Dialogic Teaching: Rethinking Classroom Talk*, 3rd edn. Thirsk: Dialogos.

Assessment Reform Group (1999). *Assessment for Learning: Beyond the Black Box*. Cambridge: Cambridge University Press.

Assessment Reform Group (2002). *Assessment for Learning: 10 Principles. Research-Based Principles to Guide Classroom Practice*. Cambridge: University of Cambridge School of Education.

Assessment Reform Group (2008). *Changing Assessment Practice: Process, Principles and Students*. London: Assessment Reform Group.

Barth, R. S. (1991). *Improving Schools from Within: Teachers, Parents, and Principals Can Make a Difference*. San Francisco, CA: Jossey-Bass.

Beere, J. (2012). *The Perfect (Ofsted) Lesson*. Carmarthen: Independent Thinking Press.

Biggs, J. B. and Collis, K. F. (1982). *Evaluating the Quality of Learning: The SOLO Taxonomy*. New York: Academic Press.

Black, P., Harrison, C., Lee, C., Marshall, B. and Wiliam, D. (2002). *Working Inside the Black Box: Assessment for Learning in the Classroom*. London: NFER Nelson.

Black, P. and Wiliam, D. (1998). *Inside the Black Box: Raising Standards through Classroom Assessment*. London: GL Assessment.

Boekaerts, M. (1995). *Motivation in Education*. London: British Psychological Society.

Boekaerts, M. (2002). *Motivation to Learn* (Educational Practices Series). International Academy of Education/ UNESCO.

Butler, R. (1988) Enhancing and Undermining Intrinsic Motivation, *British Journal of Educational Psychology*. 58 1-14.

Broughton, T. and Beere, J. (2013) *The Perfect Teacher Coach*. Carmarthen: Crown House Publishing.

Centre for the Use of Research and Evidence in Education (CUREE) [n.d.]. *Mentoring and Coaching CPD Capacity Building Project: National Framework for Mentoring and Coaching*. Available at http://www.curee-paccts.com/files/publication/1219313968/mentoring_and_coaching_national_framework.pdf (accessed 1 October 2012).

Clarke, S. (2008). *Active Learning through Formative Assessment*. London: Hodder Education.

Creemers, B.P.M. (1994) *The Effective Classroom*. London: Cassell.

Cook, V. (2000). *Second Language Learning and Language Teaching (2nd edn)*. Beijing: Foreign Language Teaching and Research Press.

De Bono, E. (1995). *Serious Creativity: Using the Power of Lateral Thinking to Create New Ideas*. London: HarperCollins.

Department for Children, Schools and Families (2009). *Improving Subject Pedagogy through Lesson Study: Handbook for Leading Teachers in Mathematics and English*. Ref: 00937-2009BKT-EN. Available at https://www.education.gov.uk/publications/eOrderingDownload/Improving%20subject%20pedagogy%20through%20Lesson%20Study.pdf (accessed 1 October 2012).

Department for Education (2007). *Assessment for Learning: 8 Schools Project Report. Secondary National Strategy for School Improvement*. Ref: 00067-2007BKT-EN. Available at http://dera.ioe.ac.uk/7600/1/1f1ab286369a7ee24df53c863a72da97-1.pdf (accessed 1 October 2012).

Department for Education (2008). *The assessment for Learning Strategy*. Ref: 00341-2008OOM-EN. Availabale at http://www.education.gov.uk/publications/standard/publicationDetail/Page1/DCSF-00341-2008 (accessed 1 October 2012).

Desforges, C. (1989). *Testing and Assessment*. London: Cassell Education.

Drummond, M. J. (1994). *Assessing Children's Learning*. London: David Fulton.

Dryden, G. and Vos, J. (2001). *The Learning Revolution: To Change the Way the World Learns* (Visions of Education). Stafford: Network Educational Press.

Dweck, C. (1986). Motivational Process Affecting Learning, *American Psychologist* 41(10), 1040–1048.

Dweck, C. (2007). *Mindset: The New Psychology of Success*. New York: Ballantine Books.

Friedman, M. (2005). *Trying Hard is Not Good Enough*. Oxford: Trafford Publishing.

Galton, M. and Williamson, J. (1992). *Group-Work in the Primary School*. London: Routledge.

Gilbert, I. (2007). *The Little Book of Thunks: 260 Questions to Make Your Brain Go Ouch!* (Independent Thinking Series). Carmarthen: Crown House Publishing.

Ginnis, P. (2001). *The Teacher's Toolkit*. Carmarthen: Crown House Publishing.

Hanson, F. A. (1994). *Testing: Social Consequences of the Examined Life*. CA: University of California Press.

Harris, A. (2002). *School Improvement: What's In It for Schools?* London: Routledge-Falmer.

Hattie, J. (2008). *Visible Learning: A Synthesis of Over 800 Meta-Analyses Relating to Achievement*. Abingdon: Routledge.

Bibliography

Hattie, J. and Timperley, H. (2007). The Power of Feedback, *Review of Educational Research* 77(1), 81–112.

Joyce, B. R. and Showers, B. (1995). *Student Achievement through Staff Development*. White Plains, NY: Longman.

Kagan, S. and Kagan, M. (2009). *Kagan Cooperative Learning*, 2nd edn. San Clemente, CA: Kagan Publishing.

Kelly, B. (2003). *Worth Repeating: More Than 5000 Classic and Contemporary Quotes*. Grand Rapids, MI: Kregel Publications.

Leahy, S., Lyon, C., Thompson, M. and Wiliam D. (2005). Classroom assessment: Minute by minute, day by day. *Educational Leadership* 63(3): 9–24. Available at http://www.ascd.org/publications/educational-leadership/nov05/vol63/num03/Classroom-Assessment@-Minute–by-Minute,-Day-by-Day.aspx (accessed 1 October 2012).

Leahy, S. and Wiliam, D. (2010). *Embedding Formative Assessment. Professional Development Pack 2 for Schools: Teacher Learning Communities in Action*. London: Specialist Schools and Academies Trust/Schools Network [CD-ROM].

Linn, R. L. and Gronlund, N. E. (2000). *Measurement and Assessment in Teaching*, 8th edn. Upper Saddle River, NJ: Prentice Hall.

Mill, J. S. (2006 [1859]). *On Liberty*. Harmondsworth: Penguin Classics.

Ofsted (2012a). *The Evaluation Schedule for the Inspection of Maintained Schools and Academies from January 2012*. Ref. 090098. Available at http://www.aaia.org.uk/content/uploads/2011/03/The-schedule-for-the-inspection-of-maintained-schools-and-academies-from-January-2012.pdf (accessed 1 October 2012).

Ofsted (2012b). *The Framework for School Inspection from September 2012*. Ref: 120100. Available at http://www.ofsted.gov.uk/resources/framework-for-school-inspection-january-2012 (accessed 1 October 2012).

Ofsted (2012c). *School inspection handbook*. Ref 120101. Available at http://www.ofsted.gov.uk/resources/school-inspection-handbook-september-2012 (accessed 14 November 2012).

Position Paper on Assessment for Learning (2009). *Paper presented at the Third International Conference on Assessment for Learning*, Dunedin, New Zealand.

Rowntree, D. (1987). *Assessing Students: How Shall We Know Them?* London: Kogan Page.

Royal Shakespeare Company (2010). *The RSC Shakespeare Toolkit for Teachers*. London: Methuen Drama.

Stewart, W. (2012). Think You've Implemented Assessment for Learning?, *TES Magazine* (13 July). Available at http://www.tes.co.uk/article.aspx?storycode=6261847 (accessed 1 October 2012).

Bibliography

Stobart, G. (2008). *Testing Times: The Uses and Abuses of Assessment*. Abingdon: Routledge.

Tofler, A. (1973). *Future Shock*. London: Pan Books.

Tuck, V. (2009). Eradicating Word Poverty; Building Word Wealth, *Daily Telegraph* (15 May). Available at http://www.telegraph.co.uk/education/vicky-tuck/5330565/Eradicating-word-poverty-building-word-wealth.html (accessed 1 October 2012).

Walters, H., Mackie, P., Mackie, R. and Bacon, A. (1997). *Global Challenge: Leadership Lessons from 'The World's Toughest Yacht Race'*. Lewes: Book Guild.

Weeden, P., Winter, J. and Broadfoot, P. (2002). *Assessment for Learning: What's In It for Schools?* London: Routledge-Falmer.

More Perfect Books ...

The Perfect Ofsted Lesson Revised and Updated by
Jackie Beere ISBN 9781781350881

The Perfect (Ofsted) Inspection by Jackie Beere
edited by Ian Gilbert ISBN 9781781350003

The Perfect (Ofsted) English Lesson by David Didau
edited by Jackie Beere ISBN 9781781350522

The Perfect Teacher Coach by Jackie Beere and
Terri Broughton edited by ISBN 9781781350034

The Perfect Teacher by Jackie Beere ISBN 9781781351000

The Perfect SENCO by Natalie Packer edited by Jackie
Beere ISBN 9781781351048

The Perfect Tutor by Jamie Flanagan Williams
edited by Jackie Beere ISBN 9781781351024

The Perfect ICT Lesson by Mark Anderson
edited by Jackie Beere ISBN 9781781351031

The Perfect (Ofsted) School Governor by Tim Bartlett
edited by Jackie Beere ISBN 9781781350904

 Bringing together some of the most innovative practitioners working
in education today under the guidance of Ian Gilbert, founder of
Independent Thinking Ltd. www.independentthinkingpress.com